———

#EatForThePlanet

Editor: Samantha Weiner
Designer: Najeebah Al-Ghadban
Production Manager: Kathleen Gaffney

Library of Congress Control Number: 2017949399

ISBN: 978-1-4197-2910-2
eISBN: 978-1-68335-230-3

Text and illustrations copyright © 2018 Nil Zacharias
and Gene Stone

Cover © 2018 Abrams

Printed and bound in the United States
10 9 8 7 6 5 4 3 2 1

Abrams Image books are available at special discounts when
purchased in quantity for premiums and promotions as well
as fundraising or educational use. Special editions can also
be created to specification. For details, contact specialsales@
abramsbooks.com or the address below.

ABRAMS The Art of Books
195 Broadway, New York, NY 10007
abramsbooks.com

#EatForThePlanet

Saving the World, One Bite at a Time

By Nil Zacharias and Gene Stone

ABRAMS IMAGE, NEW YORK

Introduction

If you picked up this book, you're probably someone who cares about the environment. You recycle your household goods. You hesitate before taking that next plane trip because of its carbon footprint. You ride a bike, walk, or use public transportation whenever possible rather than hopping into your car. You never litter. You refill your favorite water bottle from the tap. You go paperless whenever you can. You join marches. You sign petitions. You vote for politicians based on their green credentials. You've even looked into how to make your animal companion more ecologically sound—reusable bags, checking labels, using eco-friendly accessories.

But look closer, are you really so eco-friendly after all?

Even as you read this, you're thinking about that cheeseburger you're going to eat tonight. Yesterday, you had a steak. This morning, you had bacon and eggs. Setting aside the health issues these raise for you, have you stopped to consider how your food choices affect the health of the Earth?

It's unlikely you have. Because if you were thinking about the Earth, you would think twice before eating that cheeseburger. That steak. Those eggs and bacon. Not to mention that milkshake, that clam chowder, that hot dog, and that spaghetti Bolognese from the weekend.

Seriously? you ask.

Yes. Seriously.

Imagine for a moment that you're on a journey, and you're taking what appears to be the most direct road to an intended destination. You look around and notice that everyone else seems to be on the same road. There's nothing more comforting; it's the road that seems to make the most sense. It's tried and tested and people have been on it for years, knowing that it will lead them directly toward their destinations (wherever they may be), in the safest and most efficient way possible.

What if we told you that you're already on such a road; in fact, a majority of the world's population has been traveling with you on this road for at least a century. But what if we also told you that this road is veering precariously toward the edge of a cliff? And if you, and everyone else on that road, don't realize it, you are all imperiling your future?

What is this road you're on? The road is our industrialized food system, dominated by animal agriculture. And as we amble down that road, we may be feeding ourselves, but we're also feeding our extinction.

Forget about science fiction scenarios like aliens showing up and fighting humans for control of the Earth. The real battle for the future of our planet—and the future of the human race—is being fought on your plates, multiple times a day, with every food choice you make.

Okay. Does this sound like we're being overly dramatic? Is this a well-meaning argument that falls apart upon analysis?

Nope. It is not.

Industrial animal agriculture is at the heart of the biggest problem of our time—our environmental crisis.

And this book will show you exactly why, if you care about the environment, if you care for your planet, you need to change the way you eat.

Ninety-nine percent of meat, dairy, and eggs available in the United States come from the industrial animal agriculture system, or from factory farms.[1]

By eating those foods, you are doing as much, if not more, harm to the environment as if you didn't recycle, take a plane, drive your car, or find a way to make your dog your ecological statement.

But, you say, if that were true, wouldn't someone have already told you this?

Maybe they have. But maybe you haven't grasped the severity of the predicament we're in.

Earth is born

4.5 billion years ago

3 billion years ago

2 billion years ago

Human population reaches 7.5 billion

Human population reaches 1 billion

1 billion years ago

Humankind comes into the picture

200,000 years ago

200 years ago

Today

First, how did we get here?

The Earth is 4.5 billion years old, and modern humans have been on the planet for about 200,000 years or so.[2] From an ecological standpoint, things on planet Earth were relatively stable with humans in the mix for thousands of years, but that has changed drastically in the last 200 years.

The two big factors that triggered this change are the exponential growth of the human population, coupled with the rapid rise of new technology. Think about this fact for a moment: It took nearly 200,000 years for the human population to reach 1 billion, and only 200 more years to swell to 7.5 billion. In that time period, technology evolved as well and hand-driven methods of extracting resources from the earth were replaced with machine-driven methods. This is true across a wide range of industries— from textile manufacturing to coal mining.

This shift from humans coexisting with nature and using rudimentary tools to exerting complete control over the natural world and using complex machines sent us down an inevitable, yet dangerous path. For example, we've gone from fire and axes, which were some of the earliest technologies used to clear forests for farming, to multifunctional forest-eliminating machines that fell, de-limb, and stack trees for transport.

When humankind began to extract resources from our environment using technology, we had little notion of its effects on planetary ecosystems, and, in turn, humanity. So we forged ahead with the goal of improving the quality of human life in the short-term, without thinking, or knowing, about long-term consequences.

We also find ourselves with a global economic system that is dependent upon immediate rewards rather than long-term goals. This means efforts to create profits often result in a disregard for the environment. However, we can only keep tugging at the threads of our ecological tapestry for so long before it finally starts to show signs of coming unraveled.

That's where we find ourselves in the twenty-first century.

But what does your diet have to do with this, you might ask. Well, everything. Agriculture has been completely transformed in the past 200 years. Humankind decided it would be a great idea to turn farms into factories with one simple goal: to produce massive quantities of meat, eggs, and milk at the lowest possible cost.

As the world's population ballooned, factory farming rapidly emerged to feed it. Global meat production has increased more than five-fold since 1950, and large-scale, intensive livestock products has started to spread to the developing world to meet the rising demand for cheap meat and other animal products, due to factory farming becoming increasingly globalized.[3] Additionally, thanks to government subsidies that encourage overproduction (particularly in

Causes & Effects

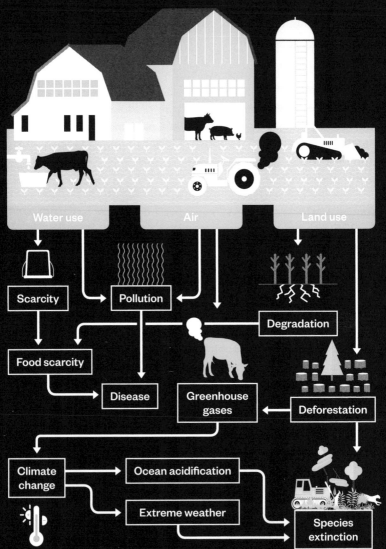

America and Western Europe), meat has become cheaper over the years, but all this progress has come with a significant cost to the planet, and to us.

You won't hear much about it in the news, but industrial animal agriculture currently occupies more than half of the world's arable land resources, uses the majority of our freshwater stores, and expels more greenhouse gas emissions than the entire transportation sector. Additionally, it causes rampant air and water pollution, land degradation, and deforestation, and is pushing countless species to the brink of extinction.

As the world's population is expected to grow to 9.8 billion by 2050, today's version of animal agriculture will likely push our planet's finite resources to their furthest limits.

To make matters worse, the growing demand for meat, eggs, and dairy—particularly in countries like China and India—is adding pressure on our current inefficient and unsustainable global food system. If we don't change course very soon, we won't be able to produce enough food for all these new people without degrading land, water, biodiversity, and the climate on a global scale. We're basically heading toward a future of potential food,[4] energy,[5] and water shortages,[6] as well as complete ecosystem collapse.[7]

That is, unless we all get off the road we've been traveling on and find a safer, more environmentally friendly path.

"It has become appallingly obvious that our technology has exceeded our humanity."

Albert Einstein

Chapter One

THIS LAND WAS MADE FOR YOU AND ME . . . AND ANIMALS, TOO

ISSUES OF LAND

How good are you at geography? Don't worry. No matter what
you think the world looks like, you've probably not seen one
that looks like this. That's because the system we depend
upon to feed our human population is largely invisible to the
people who benefit most from it.

Say hello to the new planet Earth.

Seventy-one percent of our planet is covered with water.
But you probably knew that already.

What you didn't know is that nearly half of the land that
composes the rest of this beautiful planet consists of farm
animals and crops that feed these animals.

And what you're about to learn is that this system of
agriculture isn't just destroying our planetary ecosystems—
it is changing the face of the planet itself.

45% of the planet's land surface is occupied by the global industrial livestock system.

If you really want to understand how the planet Earth came to look like this, all you need to know is that it takes 160 times more land resources to produce beef[8] than it does to produce vegetables, fruits, and legumes. But that's not where the story ends. Even chickens, pigs, dairy cows, and the other farm animals that make up our current farming system require a lot of space. After all, the livestock population is made up of more than 20 billion animals[9] (including an unbelievable 19 billion chickens!), while the human population is 7.5 billion. When you take this into account, it's not really surprising that the entire livestock system currently occupies 45 percent of the planet's land surface.[10] In comparison, 95 percent of the human population occupies 10 percent of the world's land.[11]

Human Population vs. Livestock Population

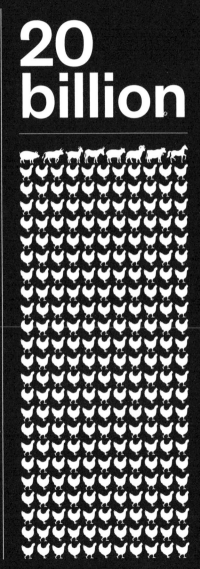

20
billion

7.5
billion

Four Unusual Ways Industrial Animal Agriculture Contributes to Climate Change

1. Livestock Respiration

Just like humans, livestock breathe in oxygen and breathe out carbon dioxide. This may not seem significant, but consider that there are approximately 20 billion-plus farm animals living and breathing at any moment worldwide. A Worldwatch Institute report noted that "a molecule of CO_2 exhaled by livestock is no more natural than one from an auto tailpipe . . . Today, tens of billions more livestock are exhaling CO_2 than in preindustrial days . . ."[12]

2. Burps and Farts

Cows, goats, and sheep are ruminants, which means they have to regurgitate and re-chew their food several times. This requires massive amounts of bacteria, which create a by-product called methane— a greenhouse gas 23 times more potent than CO_2.[13] A 2008 study found that the U.S. creates 49 million tons of methane every year, mostly from livestock.[14] At the rate that meat and dairy consumption is increasing, the Food and Agriculture Organization of the United Nations estimates that methane emissions could increase 60 percent by 2030.[15]

3. Manure

The 2.7 trillion pounds of manure produced by farm animals in the U.S.[16] is teeming with nitrous oxide (N_2O), a greenhouse gas 296 times more warming than CO_2,[17] and which lingers in the atmosphere for 150 years.[18] The United Nations Food and Agriculture Organization calculates that 65 percent of N_2O emissions are the result of livestock activities.[19] Most N_2O comes from the production of livestock feed, as well as managing livestock waste with nitrogen-based fertilizers.

4. Transportation

The billions of farm animals raised and killed each year need to be transported by trucks from farms to slaughterhouses to grocery stores. When combined with all other sources of animal agriculture greenhouse gas emissions, the Worldwatch Institute estimates that the livestock sector is responsible for 51 percent of all human-caused greenhouse gases.[20]

As the human appetite for meat, dairy, and eggs increased over the years, so did our dependence on an industrialized farming system that has livestock as its core commodity. One obvious drawback of relying on a system comprised of billions of living beings to feed our population is that those animals need to be fed as well. Additionally, raising livestock is not a short-term commitment, as most farming requires animals to be raised over months or years before they are ready to be slaughtered for meat. Or, alternatively, animals that are raised to produce milk or eggs must be kept alive for much longer. This requires a tremendous amount of livestock feed, resulting in 33 percent of arable land on the planet being used for its production.[21]

Thus began our quest to find more pasture land to increase agricultural output. Feed producers resorted to creating pastures out of grasslands and woodlands, and our forests paid the price. As of 2012, there were around 800 million acres of forest in the U.S.[22] Currently, 260 million acres (and counting) of U.S. forests have been clear-cut to create land used to produce livestock feed,[23] and 80 percent of the deforestation in the Amazon rainforest is attributed to beef production.[24]

So, what do we get out of this deal? At the cost of one acre of land, we get a yield of 250 pounds of beef. Sounds like a lot, considering you can get around 1,000 quarter-pound hamburger patties per acre.

However, the same amount of land can produce 50,000 pounds of tomatoes; up to 40,000 pounds of potatoes; 30,000 pounds of carrots; or 20,000 pounds of apples.[25]

It no longer seems like such a great use of space, does it?

Pounds per Acre

Tomatoes

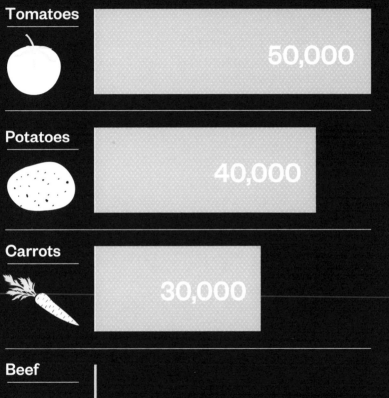

50,000

Potatoes

40,000

Carrots

30,000

Beef

250

We're replacing forests
with factory farms, thereby
exacerbating the impact
of climate change.

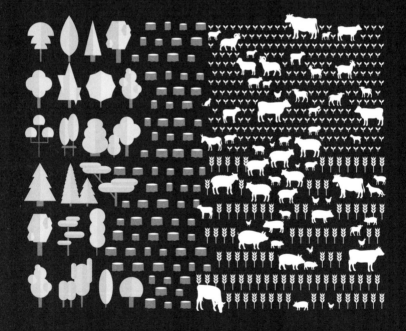

While humans might not seem to rely on trees for shelter and food in the same manner that wild animals do, our survival hinges on the health of the forests just as much as any other animal's. Trees play a vital role in balancing and maintaining the world's ecosystems. When the trees go, we lose a lot more than wood. Forests absorb massive amounts of carbon dioxide and may well be our best defense against climate-change-causing greenhouse gas emissions.

By clearing forest areas, we are not only cutting down our defenses but also releasing all of the carbon stored by those trees back into the atmosphere.

To make matters worse, we're replacing the forests with the industrial livestock system, which further exacerbates the impact on surrounding ecosystems and releases more greenhouse gases. How? Because of respiratory and digestive emissions from livestock[26] and manure management, producing feed for livestock, as well as processing and transporting the end products, which we'll cover in more detail in Chapter 4.

· What happens in the case of a few years
of bad harvests, etc.? There is no source of
food to fall back on

In order to sustain the 9.8 billion people who are predicted to
inhabit the Earth by 2050,[27] the amount of land designated
for food production will need to increase significantly. Come
2050, there's just not going to be enough land to contain and
support the human population, our food, and our food's food.
In fact, to have any hope of feeding our population, we'll need
50 percent MORE land.

As we attempt to create more pasture land, we will continue
to destroy what's left of our forests. In addition, we will try
to squeeze more output out of arable land using fertilizers,
herbicides, and pesticides until the fertile soil we rely on to
grow food is completely devoid of any nutrients. This nutrient-
deficient, dry soil will erode, with all the chemicals embedded
in it flowing with the runoff water into neighboring rivers and
lakes. Thanks to toxic chemicals, not only will aquatic life in
these water systems stand very little chance of survival, but
the wildlife that depends on that clean water will also suffer.

But plants and animals are not the only ones who will pay the
price. Eventually, violent conflicts will erupt over control of
the remaining land capable of producing fresh food as well as
the distribution of such food. Food shortages and, ultimately,
a global hunger crisis will cause these conflicts to eventually
escalate into all-out global war and mass migration as
countries grapple with the challenge of feeding their
growing yet starving populations.[28]

· Why will all of this man's magical
veggies not need pesticides and
fertilizers?

If the world's population decided to change the way it eats starting today, we could make a tremendous impact. By simply replacing our consumption of industrial meat with plant-based foods, a Dutch study predicts that roughly 10.4 million square miles (an area about the size of Africa) of grazing land would be immediately available, as well as 386,000 square miles of land that are currently being used to grow crops for livestock.[29] This land could then be converted back into grasslands and forests, by planting trees and with habitat restoration efforts, thereby helping balance carbon dioxide levels in the atmosphere and slowing down the pace of climate change.

However, returning the land lost to grazing and food production will be just the starting point. By ceasing to be reliant upon industrial animal agriculture to produce meat, dairy, and other animal products, we can also free up agricultural land that is currently occupied by vast factories that confine hundreds of thousands of animals. As the world changes the way it eats, the liberation of land from the clutches of the industrial livestock system will eventually help radically transform our planet. And as the human population grows, we will be able to produce enough healthy, nutritious food for everyone, while helping to restore our failing ecosystems.

Chapter Two

H₂ UH-OH

ISSUES OF WATER

There is a very good reason that the old adage goes, "Water is life." Every living organism on Earth requires water at some point in its life—the world's 7.5 billion people would not be able to survive without it.

Seventy-one percent of the Earth's surface is water,[30] but humans and all the other species that require freshwater to live are being hit with the harsh reality that freshwater is indeed a finite resource . . . and we're running out of it.

Only about 2.5 percent of water on the planet's surface is fresh—and just about 1 percent of that freshwater is readily accessible for human consumption[31] (i.e., only 0.3 percent of all water; the rest is locked up in glaciers and snow fields[32]). And here's where things get even stickier: Although we think of drinking water and personal hygiene as the main uses for freshwater, it's also the lynchpin of successful agriculture.

Water means life largely because water means the ability to grow food. Knowing this—and knowing that our population is continually increasing—it might seem obvious that we should work hard to make the most efficient use of water in agriculture. Unfortunately, that's not the current state of affairs.

Of the world's
7.5 billion people,
700 million
people suffer
from water
scarcity[33]
while 23% of
the planet's
freshwater
is devoted to
livestock.

Livestock is the largest beneficiary of our scarce freshwater supplies, because in order to produce meat and dairy, we need to grow a great deal of food to feed our food. And the system that's been passed down and industrialized over recent generations wastes a whole lot of that water.

- The water isn't just dissapearing, water is a renewable resource. All the water in and devoted to beef is eventually returned to the earth

Let's start with a close look at the relationship between meat and water.

Every hamburger, chicken nugget, and slab of pork starts with the same basic ingredients: corn and soy. In 2016, around 4.6 billion animals were raised and slaughtered for meat in the United States alone.[34] The only way to keep all these animals fed while keeping the price for consumers low is to feed them cheap food that fattens them up as soon as possible. Enter corn and soybeans.

In the U.S., 47 percent of soy and 60 percent of corn is consumed by livestock.[35] These crops require a great deal of water to grow: It takes about 147 gallons of water to produce 1 pound of corn[36] and 220 gallons of water to produce 1 pound of soy.[37] An average cow will consume around 1,000 pounds of feed every few months until it reaches slaughter weight (which takes between two and three years). Within a short lifetime, that cow will use about 183,500 gallons of water through feed alone.[38]

That is an exorbitant amount of water for one animal, but as they say: It ain't over 'til it's over. A cow's water footprint doesn't end with feed. Millions more gallons per animal are required for everything from hydration to washing excrement off concrete floors, cleaning blood and grease from the equipment in the butchering process, etc. (see page 95).

When all is said and done, it takes about 1,800 gallons of water on average to produce 1 pound of meat.[39] To put that into context, the average swimming pool contains 22,500 gallons of water so you could use the water needed to produce just 12.5 pounds of meat to fill an entire pool. All in all, meat is a thirsty business.

Fifteen Things You Could Do with 1,800 Gallons of Water Instead of Producing a Pound of Meat

1. Take 26 showers

2. Do 40 loads of laundry

3. Do 120 loads of dishes in a dishwasher

4. Flush your toilet 1,125 times

5. Produce 7 pounds of tofu

6. Grow 12 pounds of avocados

7. Grow 53 pounds of potatoes

8. Grow 13 pounds of wheat

9. Grow 21 pounds of apples

10. Grow 4.5 pounds of rice

11. Produce 11 bottles of wine

12. Produce 5 bottles of whiskey

13. Produce 40 pints of beer

14. Manufacture 7 iPhones

15. Manufacture 1 laptop

The Average Flushing System Uses 150 Gallons of Water per Cow, per Day

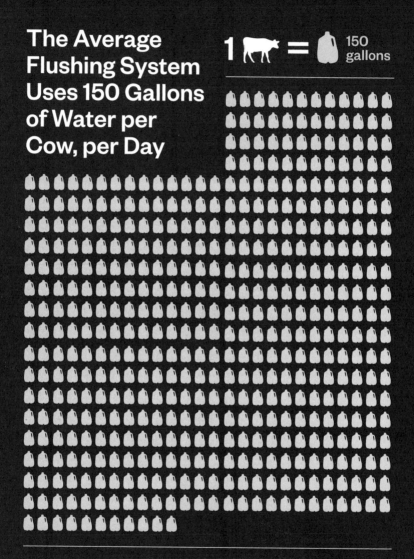

1 🐄 = 🧴 150 gallons

The above graph represents the 150 gallons per cow water usage of 475 cows (average number of cows on American farms) totaling 71,250 gallons of water per day.

Speaking of thirsty, let's turn our sights to the dairy industry to see how much water is hidden there as well.

Just as in the case of meat production, most of the water needed to produce dairy comes from manufacturing feed. In fact, 98 percent of milk's water footprint can be traced back to a cow's food,[40] and dairy cows eat a lot!

The preferred food for dairy cows is alfalfa, as cows efficiently use its high levels of protein, calcium, and high-quality fiber to produce milk. As you might imagine, constantly producing milk (the average dairy cow produces 6 to 7 gallons daily[41]) puts a huge strain on the metabolism of dairy cows, and they need to replenish that energy through their food.

Like corn and soy, alfalfa is a water-intensive crop: producing 1 pound requires around 114 gallons of water.[42] This is a better water-to-feed ratio than corn or soy, but dairy cows need around 6 pounds of alfalfa to produce 1 gallon of milk. If a dairy cow is producing 7 gallons of milk a day, that totals out to 4,788 gallons of water . . . per cow . . . per day.

Alfalfa is an incredible crop for field rotation and will often grow with no overview of the farmer

At the risk of sounding redundant, food is only one part of a dairy cow's water footprint. Cows also drink around 23 gallons of water a day[43] just to stay hydrated (for context, a well-hydrated person drinks about 1 gallon of water daily).

This means you can tack on an additional 10,925 gallons of water to the aforementioned dairy farm's water footprint.

Now that we've handled food and water, let's talk sanitation.

Milk and cheese production is a messy endeavor. The average mid-size dairy factory farm houses between 200 and 700 cows, all of which have to crowd into a milking parlor multiple times a day. Between the excrement produced by these animals and the literal spilled milk, keeping a parlor floor clean requires a huge amount of water. Most farms have automated flushing systems that use an average of 150 gallons of water per cow, per day.[44] In total, a farm with 475 cows could use 71,250 gallons per day on flushing systems alone.

All things considered, by the time that gallon of milk makes it to your refrigerator, around the same amount of water that you use for a whole month's worth of showers—about 2,000 gallons—has been used in its creation. So, if you're looking to conserve water, you may want to reconsider your weekly gallon of milk.

What does all this mean in terms of an individual's water footprint? An estimated 4,200 gallons of water per day[45] is required to produce the average diet that contains meat and dairy.

According to the United States Environmental Protection Agency, an average family of four uses about 400 gallons of water a day[46] for various indoor activities, including taking showers, washing dishes, doing laundry, and flushing the toilet. This statistic, however, doesn't take into consideration how our food consumption affects our water footprint. If each member of this hypothetical family of four ate a cheeseburger for dinner, that household's daily water consumption would shoot up to over 7,000 gallons[47] (depending on the size of the burgers, the amount of cheese, etc.).

Average Household Water Use

Average Household Water Use Including Cheeseburgers

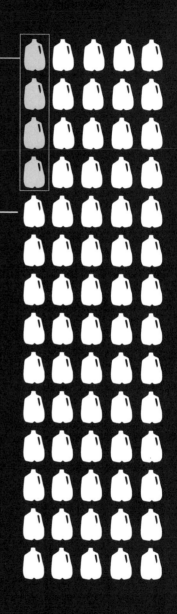

 = 100 gallons

In 1 year, the average American consumes roughly 58 pounds of beef, 50 pounds of pork, and 91 pounds of chicken.[48]

The water that it takes to produce just a pound of each one of these meats is approximately 1,800 gallons, 576 gallons, and 468 gallons, respectively.[49] To put this into perspective, it only takes 119 gallons of water to produce 1 pound of potatoes.[50]

Simply stated, if we used all of this water to produce food for direct human consumption, rather than the roundabout process of industrial meat farming, we would have a lot more food and a whole lot more water to go around.

About 800 million people worldwide currently lack access to clean water,[51] and a total of 2.7 billion people find water scarce for at least one month of the year.[52] By 2025, two-thirds of the world's population may face water shortages,[53] and climate change will only exacerbate the problem as it alters rainfall patterns. And all the while, we have that water—and we are using it for burgers.

wtf is your plan to get the people needing water the water from a cow's trough? They don't have water bc they live in literal fucking deserts

and yet growing potatoes destroys farm fields when over used

How Much Americans Eat Annually:

Beef
54 pounds

Pork
46 pounds

Chicken
83 pounds

Potato
142 pounds[54]

How Much Water It Takes to Produce a Pound of Each:

 **1,800 gallons**

 **576 gallons**

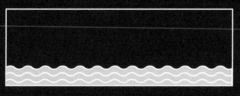 **468 gallons**

119 gallons

Drought will no longer be considered a temporary emergency if we do not change our eating habits. It will, instead, become the universal norm. By 2025, over half of the world's population will face water shortages. By 2050, up to 75 percent of people will be in a state of water scarcity.[55] Taps will run dry. Reservoirs will be a luxury of the past.

We'll have drilled so deep into the Earth's bedrock to retrieve ancient water stores that the sinkholes we're seeing in Florida today will seem like small puddles. Due to extreme water shortages, all supplies will become privatized and freshwater will no longer be a human right—it will be a commodity valued more highly than gold.

Many people found it absurd when restaurants in California stopped giving customers tap water unless they specifically requested it, but in the future, people may find the idea strange that we once told children to turn off the faucet when brushing their teeth, because at some point it will no longer be guaranteed that when a tap is turned on, water will even appear.

Not only will domestic water supplies be reduced to near zero, in some areas local waterways and lakes will all but disappear. This will not bode well for the weather system as there can be no restorative rains if there is nothing to evaporate into the atmosphere.

Clouds will be replaced with relentlessly blue skies, and future generations will know nothing of rain storms or puddles. Moreover, the plethora of freshwater marine life we know and love today will cease to exist. If we're lucky, desalinization of ocean water will be able to make up for the lack of potable water for those who can afford it. After all, there won't be any short supply of ocean water if the ice caps have all melted.

- Water from the ocean is evaporated and comes back down in clean rain water

---

- Never seems to address opposition which leads me to believe he has very few counter arguments
- Constantly sounds like a condescending prick
- Whole book thus far just seems like 4 vegans jerking each other off and patting themselves on the back
- Uses fear as a tool of motivation

Let's say you wanted to go all out and avoid animal products like meat, eggs, cheese, and milk, and instead choose a plant-based diet for just one day. By doing so, your diet would require 1,500 fewer gallons of water, which is enough to meet the daily indoor needs of approximately fifteen people in the United States. Now imagine if the entire planet made such a small yet meaningful shift away from animal-based foods! We might finally be able to give ourselves a fighting chance of combating global water shortages.

This shift has the potential to have a profound impact on our planet. First, some of the water that's currently being funneled into the livestock system would be repurposed for more useful activities that promote human health and well-being, including making water available to the 1 in 9 people around the world who currently lack access to safe drinking water. This will help slow down the rate at which we're draining our freshwater stores. Life in our rivers and lakes will recuperate, and so will wildlife surrounding these bodies of water. This change, coupled with the other downstream impacts of revamping our agricultural system, such as reduced pollution and dead zone relief, will help restore the much-needed balance in our world's ecosystems and give our growing population hope for survival.

> at a peak fucking high currently

= 100 gallons

By eating a plant-based diet, you would require 1,500 fewer gallons of water, which is enough to meet the daily indoor needs of approximately 15 people in the United States.

Chapter Three

GRAIN DRAIN

ISSUES OF FOOD

Considering all the progress we have made over the past 200 years in our methods of cultivating crops and rearing livestock—using machines and computer technology—we ought to be yielding some impressive results in food production.

In other words, shouldn't we be pretty good at feeding the world's population by now?

Well, we're not. So what's going on here?

Blame capitalism. If all of a sudden all that grain was no longer needed for livestock, the people who are poor and without food still can't afford it and still go hungry

40% of our world's grain is fed to livestock[56] while nearly **1 billion** people go to bed hungry every night.[57]

Livestock consume 80% of the global soy crop.

Twenty thousand plant species are known to be edible.[58] However, fewer than 20 species now provide 90 percent of our food,[59] and only 3 crops—rice, maize, and wheat—contribute nearly 60 percent[60] of the calories and proteins obtained by humans from plants. In general, around 75 percent of the world's food is generated from only 12 plants and 5 animal species.[61]

However, a significant portion of the calories from our staple crops are used to feed animals.

When it comes to the question of who is eating the world's grain, the answer is clear: 55 percent of crops are directly eaten by people while 36 percent go to livestock. On top of that, around 9 percent are turned into biofuels and industrial products. When it comes to corn, these animals get between 40 and 50 percent of the annual crop yield. These animals are fed grains because it facilitates rapid weight gain, readying them for slaughter more quickly.

So while we are doing an excellent job ensuring that our farm animals are fed sufficient quantities of grain to fatten them up, nearly 21,000 people die of hunger or hunger-related causes every day.[62] The root cause of these fatalities isn't a shortage of food, but rather our dependence on an unbalanced food system that is draining our natural resources to cater to the needs and tastes of only a part of the global population.

Five Reasons Why Governments around the World Decided That Growing Feed for Livestock Was More Important than Feeding Hungry People

1. You Can Feed Farm Animals Bad Food

People ask questions. Cows, pigs, and chickens don't. They don't wonder where their food comes from and willingly consume cheap corn and soy that is genetically modified, sprayed with pesticides, and designed to make them overweight and sick.

2. Monocultures Are Just Easier

Why bother growing a diverse array of crops when you can just focus on essential commodity crops like corn and soy to make up more than half of the farmland in the United States? Just keep it simple, stupid! Eighty percent of the global soybean crop and 40 to 50 percent of the annual corn crop are fed to cattle, pigs, chickens, and other animals used in agriculture. And we don't hear them complaining.

3. The Bigger the Factory Farm, the More Money to Be Made

Eating fruits and vegetables may be great for people and, in fact, recommended by health experts, but let's get real: Where's the fun in salad? And by fun, we mean money. Mega-farms have mega-money and they don't grow fruits and vegetables, so why bother funneling tax dollars in the form of subsidies for healthy crops when you can help the rich get richer? And what are the rich great at? Coughing up millions in political campaign contributions when election time comes around. Small farmers, the health of the public, and common sense be damned. This is just easy. Notice a trend?

4. The Razor and Razorblade Strategy, Duh

When you get farmers to grow just

one or two crops on the same land and get the entire animal agriculture industry to rely on it, farmers end up with a razor that needs a steady supply of razor blades to be of any use. In farming terms, they have to rely heavily on chemicals. Namely, synthetic fertilizers, because growing the same plant on the same land year after year rapidly depletes the nutrients in the soil. In addition, you need pesticides to control weed and insect populations. And it should come as no surprise that six giant corporations dominate the world's seed and agrochemical industries. You catch our drift. Easy money.

5. An Appetite for Meat Keeps the Global Economy Booming

The bottom line is, it's a win-win strategy for all.

People in the Western world and the rising middle class in the developing world get to spend their money eating foods that make them happy (meat and cheese!), and they get to buy it for a price that's cheaper than boring salads. As the junk food industry, big meat, egg, and dairy producers, as well as the giant agrochemical and biotech companies get richer, their favorite politicians get elected into office, who in turn continue to develop policies that keep this cycle going. Most importantly, the global economy flourishes! What are the long-term consequences on human health and the environment? Hey, who has time to think about that when we have all this great food to eat?

Monocultures in the US are rare. All farmers know this is terrible so they choose to rotate fields every year with new crops and letting fields go fallow

Although crops used for animal feed are ultimately converted into human food in the form of meat, eggs, and dairy products, this is done with a substantial loss of caloric efficiency. A great deal of wastage occurs in the process of turning these crops into animal foods, and only a fraction of the calories in feed given to livestock make their way into the meat, milk, and eggs that we consume. For every 100 calories of grain fed to animals, we get only about 40 new calories of milk, 22 calories of eggs, 12 of chicken, 10 of pork, or 3 of beef.[63] Simply put, meat, dairy, and eggs are extremely inefficient ways of feeding the human population.

The world's beef-producing cattle require a quantity of food equal to the caloric needs of 8.7 billion people,[64] which is more than the entire planet's human population.

- a calorie is a calorie is a calorie?
This is an extremely short sided and illogical graphic

For every 100 calories of grain fed to animals, we get only this many new calories:

Calories:

Milk
40

Eggs
22

Chicken
12

Pork
10

Beef
3

Global hunger is a problem we actually have the power to end within a few years. The solution is one in which each of us (especially those in the Western world) can play an integral part. By shifting our diet away from animal-based foods and incorporating more foods derived from plant-based sources, we could allow the world to directly consume more of the calories produced from farming on existing cropland.

We could make around 70 percent more calories available, potentially providing enough calories to feed an additional 4 billion people, just by targeting all crop production currently used for animal feed and other non-food uses (including biofuels) for direct consumption.[65] While that's easier said than done, imagine if we could shift even half of it; we could easily grow enough food to feed everyone sustainably.

← what about the migrant workers that will have to work the fields? Vegetables take up substantially more time of actual humans than ranching or grain farming

Eight Reasons Plants Make You Healthy

A diet rich in plants will dramatically increase your intake of many important macro- and micronutrients. These include:

1. Fiber
A plant-based diet is naturally high in fiber, which means a healthier colon and digestive tract.

2. Antioxidants
Antioxidants guard against cell damage, and unlike animal-based foods, plant foods are filled with them.

3. Vitamin C
It abounds in fruits and vegetables, and will boost your immune system and, new research finds, possibly your cardiovascular health.[66]

4. Magnesium
Magnesium is essential for the absorption of calcium; it also calms nerves, relieves muscle aches, and increases energy. Found in leafy greens, nuts, and whole grains.[67]

5. Folate
One of the B vitamins, the name comes from the Latin word folium, meaning "leaf." Folate enhances the body's metabolism and promotes cellular growth. Found in legumes, nuts, seeds, and soy products.

6. Potassium
Crucial to many bodily functions, potassium keeps your body's cells, tissues, and organs healthy. It also helps your body maintain a healthy blood pH level. Abundant in beans, dark leafy greens, potatoes, mushrooms, bananas, and many other plant foods.

7. Vitamin E
This vitamin's antioxidant properties promote health in your heart, skin, eyes, and brain, and may even reduce your cholesterol levels, among many other benefits. It is best ingested from grains, nuts, and dark leafy greens.

8. Phytochemicals
These chemical compounds occur in plants ("phyto" is the Greek word for "plant") and protect them against such threats as insects and disease. Phytochemicals protect those who eat these plants as well by offering a vast range of benefits, including lowering the risk of chronic diseases. Each individual phytochemical offers its own advantages, and scientists have estimated that as many as 4,000 phytochemicals, if not more, exist[68]—that's a lot of potential benefits.

By 2050 the world's population will reach nearly 9.8 billion, with almost all of this increase taking place in developing countries. Moreover, this will be coupled with the rise of urbanization as people migrate away from rural communities to cities in search of jobs and a better standard of living. As people's income levels rise, so will the demand for food.

To meet the demands of almost ten billion people, we'll need more food in the next 40 years than was needed in the past 10,000 years, which we can't achieve with our current farming systems unless we can create more water or land.

The net result will be massive food shortages and a rise in global hunger rates. Food is obviously key to human survival, and with limited access to it, large sections of the global population will grow increasingly desperate and angry. This anger and desperation will most likely first begin to manifest itself in the form of protests, which will quickly escalate into violent riots. (When food shortages struck Venezuela in 2016, violent riots quickly ensued. Within the span of two weeks, at least fifty outbursts occurred, leading to mass destruction and fatalities.[69]) People will raid shops, farms, and homes to access staple foods like grain and salt. Within months, these riots will spread from city to city and become more organized and increasingly violent, ultimately morphing into armed conflict between organized food militias and the government.

Eventually, governments will be overthrown, violence and chaos will be the norm in urban areas, and the fight for food will extend beyond national borders and transform into global war. Millions of people will starve to death and millions more will be killed, with countries invaded and entire populations wiped out as the battle for food is waged between nations employing the fullest extent of their military might.

To meet the demands of 9.8 billion people, we'll need to produce more food in the next 40 years than has been created in the past 10,000 years combined—and it will require producing 70% more food than we do now.

Food production in the past 10,000 years

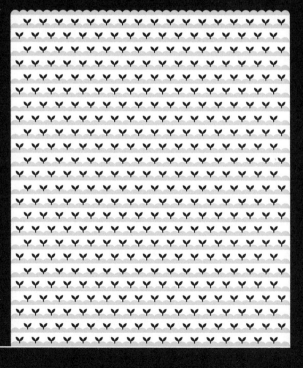

The average American consumes roughly 1,892 pounds of grain a year,[70, 71] but in the form of meat. If everyone in the country stopped eating meat today, that would mean that all of this grain could be used to feed around 1.4 billion people[72] on a plant-based diet. But remember, this is only if the 326 million people in the U.S. give up meat.

As previously mentioned, if we could shift even just half of the world's grain production from feed purposes to human uses, and convert available cropland accordingly, we could easily grow enough food sustainably to feed an additional 2 billion people.

This combined with a shift in global food distribution could ensure that people in developing countries have access to food at prices they can afford. This change could have a profound impact on the problem of global hunger. It's not only the best chance we have at feeding a population of 9.8 billion by 2050—it's our only chance.

Four Examples of How Much You Can Save by Eating Plant-Based

	Water	Grain	Forest Area	CO_2 Equivalent
In 1 Day				
	1,500 gallons	45 pounds	30 sq. feet	20 pounds
In 1 Week				
	10,500 gallons	315 pounds	210 sq. feet	140 pounds
In 1 Month				
	46,500 gallons	1,395 pounds	930 sq. feet	620 pounds
In 1 Year				
	547,500 gallons	16,425 pounds	10,950 sq. feet	7,300 pounds

Chapter Four

WHAT THE FRACK?

ISSUES OF ENERGY AND EMISSIONS

71

When it comes to being "environmentally friendly," some of the ideas that have been drilled into our collective conscious-ness over the years include the following: We need to con-serve energy at home. We need to recycle our trash. We need to reduce our reliance on gas-guzzling cars.

While none of these ideas is inherently wrong, taken together they don't paint an accurate picture of what's really suck-ing up our energy resources and wreaking havoc on global climate patterns. Let's take the last example, for instance. Hybrid and electric cars have become the new status sym-bols of the eco-minded populace. Heck, good luck trying to call yourself environmentally friendly while you cart yourself and your stuff around in a 7-seater SUV. You might as well slap on a custom license plate that says hypocrite, because nearly everyone knows that gasoline and diesel are produced by refining crude oil, a nonrenewable/finite resource. In addition, cars pollute the environment and release harmful greenhouse gas emissions that are leading to significant changes in the world's climate. Congrats, you get it! But if you are aware of the environmental impact of transportation, you ought to take your environmentally friendly journey one further step.

Here's a dirty little secret: The livestock system releases more greenhouse gases than all the world's transportation— that's all the automobiles, planes, trains, and ships— combined. In fact, emissions generated during the production of a typical 8-ounce steak are equivalent to driving a small car for about 29 miles.[73]

The livestock system is responsible for 14.5% of greenhouse gas emissions . . . that's more than the entire transportation sector combined.[74]

If you have been paying attention to the issue of climate change, you probably already know a thing or two about fossil fuels (so called because these substances were formed in the past from the remains of once-living organisms) such as coal, oil, and natural gas. Fossil fuels power a vast majority of our modern conveniences; we take them from the ground and then burn them,[75] which we have been doing since the dawn of the industrial revolution. This process has led to the release of harmful greenhouse gases, which form thick blankets over the Earth, trapping heat and causing global temperatures to rise.

Our overwhelming dependence on fossil fuels has lead to more carbon dioxide in the atmosphere today than at any time in the past 600,000 years.[76] At this rate, by the year 2100, scientists expect the Earth to be on average four degrees Celsius warmer than in preindustrial times,[77] which spells disaster for plants, animals, and humans alike.[78]

From crop to table, it takes a lot of fossil fuels to power the production processes necessary to feed our appetite for animal protein. These processes include everything from feed, transportation, and the use of synthetic fertilizers/pesticides to the staggering amount of energy it takes to power factory farms. Overall, the production of 1 calorie of animal protein requires about 10 times as much fossil fuel energy as is needed for 1 calorie of plant protein.[79] This input can be higher depending on the type of meat produced. For example, grain-fed beef requires about 35 fossil fuel calories (amount of energy expended) for every 1 calorie produced.[80]

It all starts with the food we feed to livestock. Feed production accounts for around 50 percent of the fossil fuels used in livestock production.[81, 82] America's 20,000 factory farms[83] use about 5.5 gallons of fossil fuels per acre.[84] The average farm in the United States spans 1,296 acres,[85] meaning it will devour about 7,128 gallons of fossil fuels. Burning 1 gallon of fossil fuels releases 19.6 pounds of CO_2.[86] Now consider the hundreds of millions more factory farms there are across the globe. In addition, we currently use an average of 180 million tons of synthetic, petroleum-based fertilizer to grow livestock feed. The biggest user of fossil fuel energy in industrial animal agriculture is for petrochemicals. Up to 40 percent of the energy used in the food system goes toward the production of artificial fertilizers and pesticides, which are derived from atmospheric nitrogen and natural gas.

Animal Protein vs. Plant Protein

The production of 1 calorie of animal protein requires about 10 times as much input of fossil fuel energy as is needed for 1 calorie of plant protein.

Their production and distribution takes an average of 5.5 gallons of fossil fuels per acre.[87] As the Earth's population grows and the demand for meat increases, projections indicate that we'll need 230 million tons, or 7.3 billion gallons, of fertilizer just to produce feed crops by 2050.[88]

Machinery does the bulk of the heavy lifting in factory farms. Research from Cornell University indicates that the agriculture industry uses about 17 percent of fossil fuel energy[89] in the U.S.—powering factory-farm facilities accounts for a large part of this expenditure. Just think about the amount of energy required to keep a shed filled with over 20,000 chickens cool—or the mammoth heating bill necessary to keep 30,000 pigs warm in the middle of a Midwestern winter.

Concentrated dairy operations require additional energy to power automated flushing systems that remove waste, dirt, and excess milk from the floor.

Packaging and shipping meat, dairy, and eggs to grocery stores accounts for 23 percent of the energy used in our food production system.[90] The majority of factory farms in the United States are located in the Midwest,[91] meaning that meat often has to travel long distances to reach consumers. This requires massive temperature-controlled trucks, another energy drain. (In comparison to energy needed to transport local food, non-local distribution uses 4 to 17 times more fuel.[92])

Five Ways to Reduce Your Carbon Footprint and Save Money

1. Switch to Energy-Efficient Lighting

By switching all of your lightbulbs to energy-efficient LEDs or compact fluorescents, you can save money and help the environment. Just one energy-efficient bulb can save 1,300 pounds of CO_2,[93] and if every house in America switched to compact fluorescents we could reduce the energy spent on lighting by 50 percent.

2. Unplug Electronics

Even if their displays are off, electronics are still sipping power. Unplug your TV, cable box, computer, and other devices when you are not using them and save $100 every year on your electric bill while helping the environment.

3. Drive Smartly

Electric cars and hybrids are among the best ways to reduce your carbon footprint. According to the EPA, a plug-in hybrid can save 7,000 pounds of carbon dioxide (CO_2) tailpipe emissions per year compared to a 26-mpg non-hybrid—that's equivalent to planting 79 trees.[94] But you can still reduce your emissions without a hybrid. Instead of buying a gas-guzzling SUV, use an aerodynamic hitch-mounted cargo rack on your sedan. Inflating your tires properly can save up to 3 percent on gas. Of course, the smartest way to drive is to not drive at all—use public transportation or carpool!

4. Insulate Your Home

Heating and cooling represent 50 to 70 percent of your energy costs. By properly insulating your walls and windows, you can drastically cut down on your energy usage while burning less fossil fuel. During winter, you can save an enormous amount of energy by opening your curtains during the day and closing them at night.

5. Avoid Meat and Dairy

The Worldwatch Institute estimates that 51 percent of greenhouse gas emissions are directly and indirectly caused by rearing animals for slaughter, from deforested lands to transportation costs to methane discharge.[95] (Methane, which is produced naturally by cows, is 23 times more potent than carbon dioxide.) But by now you've figured that one out.

All this adds up to a whole lot of greenhouse gas emissions. The United Nations Food and Agriculture Organization estimates that livestock production is responsible for 14.5 percent of global human-created greenhouse gas emissions,[96] while other organizations such as the Worldwatch Institute have estimated it could be as much as 51 percent.[97] This number takes into account not only the fossil fuels used to produce and transport livestock before and after slaughter, but also the other gases that livestock produce on their own.

In addition to releasing massive greenhouse gas emissions, the industrial livestock system is also leading to the decimation of our precious rainforests. The destruction of forests has ramifications far more wide-sweeping than just the loss of land. Remember the statistic mentioned earlier (page 25) that 80 percent of the deforestation currently going on in the Amazon was attributed to beef production? The canopy of trees in the Amazon acts as a giant carbon store,[98] trapping CO_2 that the trees have absorbed from the atmosphere. When we chop down those trees to clear space for livestock, we not only release all of that stored CO_2 back into the air, we remove valuable trees that would be helping to clean up the air and produce oxygen.

2,000 trees are lost to deforestation every minute, 80% of this is caused by cattle production. That means every 60 seconds, we have 1,600 fewer trees to help keep excess CO_2 from contributing to pollution and climate change.

Too much CO_2 in the air traps gases and particulates in the atmosphere, contributing to climate change[99] and pollution. It takes 9 trees 1 month[100] to scrub 10 pounds of CO_2 out of the atmosphere.

Our current trends in food production alone will cause us to reach, and possibly exceed, the world's carbon budget. This budget, if maintained, gives us a good chance of keeping global warming below the scientific community's recomended 35 degrees Fahrenheit (1.5 degrees Celsius) by 2050.[101]

Five Ways Oil Exploration in the Arctic Harms Whales

1. Hearing Loss
The seismic blasts used in exploration can be loud enough to burst human eardrums. Whales are more sensitive to sounds, and these blasts can cause temporary or permanent hearing loss, highly dangerous for a creature whose daily activities rely on echolocation.

2. Freeze and Sink Response
Narwhals are particularly susceptible to seismic blasting because they are unlikely to flee an area when faced with a threat. Instead, they have been observed to respond to loud noise by freezing and sinking, which means the whales stay near the source of a seismic blast and suffer from additional impacts, such as hearing damage and stress.

3. Ice Entrapment
Scientists have observed that narwhal migration is disrupted by seismic blasting noise, which delays their migration to a later date when ice reforms, resulting in thousands of narwhals becoming entrapped in the winter sea ice, causing them to die.

4. No More Songs
Whales are known for their vocalization, essential for their species communication. Scientific documentation shows blasting causes whales to reduce or even stop singing altogether.

5. Stress
Stress hormones in whales often increase in response to seismic noise. The effects of this stress can inhibit the immune system or otherwise compromise the health of the animals.

Greenhouse gas emissions from all food production will increase 80 percent by 2050,[102] portending disaster for the planet. Average temperatures around the world will rise and extreme weather events will become more frequent and more deadly. Some parts of the world will experience heat waves and drought, which will fuel intense wildfires, cause dust storms, and impact food production and water quality.

We're already starting to see this happen with increased instances of wildfires in California and Australia. Warming temperatures will also increase air pollution and the spread of airborne illnesses. Other parts of the world will experience severe storms and excessive rainfall, resulting in overflowing rivers and lakes, intense flooding, and damage to life and property.

This flooding will not only contaminate water supplies but lead to the spread of insects and bacteria, resulting in food and waterborne illnesses. Low-income communities, children, and the elderly will be the most affected by these severe weather events. Rising sea levels have already forced people on the Marshall Islands and Kiribati to relocate, as forecasts indicate that their entire countries will be completely submerged within five decades.[103, 104, 105]

The rising levels of greenhouse gas emissions will also have a huge impact on our oceans. The oceans absorb about 30 percent of the carbon dioxide released into the atmosphere,[106] and higher levels of emissions will increase acidification, devastating entire marine ecosystems that humans depend upon. In addition, the world's ice sheets will melt, increasing sea levels and causing massive flooding in coastal regions and low-lying areas, including entire island nations. The world's largest cities, like New York, Sydney, and Mumbai, will be among the first to be impacted. The rising sea levels and the resulting threat to life and property, along with food and water shortages, will cause mass migration of people and spur an international refugee crisis involving millions of people. This will only accelerate security threats around the world by provoking conflicts over land and resources that will eventually escalate to global war.

The monetary losses suffered as a result of war and property damage will be monumental, eventually crippling the world's economy to the point of collapse.

By shifting to a diet primarily comprised of plant-based foods, you can cut your carbon footprint in half. The resulting benefit to the world would be immense. According to one study,[107] by transitioning toward a diet that is predominantly plant-based/vegetarian, we could reduce global mortality by 6 to 10 percent, food-related greenhouse gas emissions by 29 to 70 percent, and the economic benefits of the change could be 1 to 31 trillion dollars by midcentury, thanks to fewer damaging environmental impacts, premature deaths worldwide, and lost working days, as well as reduced health care costs.

This shift would play a huge role in slowing climate change. As temperatures around the world stabilized, eventually extreme weather events would become a thing of the past.[108] Soil, air, freshwater, and forests would begin to steadily show signs of repair as the weather equilibrated. Ocean acidification would slow down marine ecosystems would start to bounce back, and the severe devastation expected to hit coastal regions, low-lying areas, and entire island nations would be prevented or delayed. Eventually, the sea level and ocean surface temperatures would return to preindustrial levels.

We may not be able to halt the path of climate change, but we may be able to slow it down to manageable levels, where communities, economies, and ecosystems can adapt and thereby ensure long-term survival of the human species.

Five Reasons Why We Shouldn't Frack

1. Water Pollution

To create fissures in rock formations, millions of gallons of water, sand, and a chemical cocktail (including formaldehyde, acetic acid, and boric acid to name a few) are put into wells at very high pressures. Depending on the geology of the area, between 25 and 75 percent of this contaminated water returns to the surface as wastewater that is then collected and injected deep underground. This water is highly toxic and more often than not finds its way into aquifers and surface water or seeps into soil.

2. Negative Effects on Human Health

Twenty-five percent of fracking fluid is composed of known carcinogens and chemicals that can migrate into public waters. In Pennsylvania and Wyoming, benzene and methane was found in groundwater and aquifers used for drinking water. Fracking also releases ionizing radiation from naturally occurring radium-226, and exposure to this sort of radiation has been linked to breast cancer.

3. Negative Impact on Animal Health

The U.S. Geological Survey reports that of the 750 chemicals used in fracking, more than 100 are EDCs (Endocrine Disrupting Chemicals) that have been linked to respiratory, gastrointestinal, neurological, and reproductive conditions. EDCs have been linked to sex changes in wildlife, and contaminated waters have also caused fish deaths in Pennsylvania.

4. Threat to Farmers

In the Marcellus Shale region of Pennsylvania, many farmers are being asked to lease their land to gas companies for fracking. While most farmers own their land rights, the mineral rights associated with the shale the farms sit on top of are up for grabs. Unable to afford lawyers to sue gas companies for the mineral rights to their land, farmers have been forced to abandon their farms. Farmers who do stay in areas that have begun fracking risk losing crops and livestock to fracking fluid contamination.

5. The Many Things We Still Don't Know

The fact is, we still don't really know what potential effect fracking can have on the planet.

Chapter Five

TOXIC SHOCKS

ISSUES OF AIR AND WATER POLLUTION

"Where there's life, there's poop." Perhaps this isn't a famous saying yet, but it should be, because poop, like death and taxes, is an absolute certainty. The billions of animals who feed humans, and the food that feeds those animals, occupy nearly 45 percent of the planet's land surface,[109] presenting a rather interesting challenge of waste management and disposal.

Yes, all those mega-factories where thousands of animals are packed in for the purpose of mass-producing food also produce some mega-amounts of feces . . . mountains of poop are crammed into cesspools that measure several football fields long. And guess what? We don't have some other planet we can send these feces off to.

An average beef cow can eat around 90 pounds of food daily and poop 15 times a day, producing about 65 pounds of feces, totaling about 12 tons of feces in a year.[110] A lactating dairy cow, on the other hand, can produce as much as 150 pounds of poop every day,[111] which amounts to more than 27 tons a year. You get the picture.

• This is reused as fertilizer

Livestock in the U.S. produce 396 million tons of excrement every year. That's enough poop to fill the entire Empire State Building every single day of the year.

Now think about the fact that the population of industrial farm animals around the world is almost 20 billion (according to estimates from the U.N. Food and Agriculture Organization).[112] Livestock in the U.S. alone produce 369 million tons of excrement every year.[113] That's enough poop to fill the entire Empire State Building every single day of the year. This is far more waste than all the farms in the U.S. could ever redistribute as fertilizer, so the majority of it is allowed to fester in massive, open-air waste lagoons.[114] This waste is a pollutant,[115] not a productive farming tool as some might believe.

got me there

These enormous cesspools release around 400 different harmful gases into the atmosphere. These gases include nitrous oxide, methane, carbon dioxide, ammonia, and hydrogen sulfide.[116] In fact, around 80 percent of ammonia emissions in the U.S. come from farm animal waste.[117] You've probably come into contact with ammonia in cleaning products—and if you have, you are familiar with the health warnings that adorn the side of the spray bottles. Its effects include dizziness, eye irritation, respiratory illness, and nausea.

In addition to ammonia, factory farm waste releases dangerous levels of hydrogen sulfide. Exposure to this gas, even in small doses, can cause sore throats, seizures, comas, and even death.[118] When it mixes into the atmosphere, hydrogen sulfide reacts with oxygen to make sulfuric acid, which can return to the Earth's surface in the form of acid rain.

While adults are highly susceptible to these toxic gases, children, who take in 20 to 50 percent more air than adults,[119] are at extreme risk of experiencing these adverse effects. Kids raised in communities near factory farms are more likely to develop asthma or bronchitis.[120] Low air quality can also exacerbate asthma symptoms.

Four Reasons Farmed Fish Are Not Healthy

Today, nearly half of the world's seafood comes from fish farms, also known as aquaculture. You might think that eating farmed fish is better for the planet than eating wild-caught fish, which are dangerously overexploited. You would be wrong.

1. Depletion of Prey Fish

Some farmed fish are fed soy or corn, but many species, such as salmon, require a more natural diet of small prey fish. To feed farmed fish, commercial fishers have drastically depleted herring and anchovy stocks, the latter of which the U.N. calls "the most heavily exploited fish in world history."[121]

2. Farmed Fish Spread Disease to Wild Fish

Many fish farms are built inside oceans, rivers, and other natural waterways. Diseases such as sea lice, salmon leukemia virus, and piscine reovirus are rampant among genetically modified farmed fish and can easily penetrate permeable barriers. Some studies have found that salmon farming can reduce the survival rates of nearby wild populations by 50 percent or more.[122]

3. Pollution

A report commissioned by the global nonprofit the World Wide Fund for Nature found that Scottish fish farms produce more nutrient pollution than Scotland's entire human pollution.[123] The problem is mainly nitrogen and phosphorus, which promote toxic algae blooms that deplete oxygen and kill wildlife.

4. Fish Farms Kill Coral Reefs

Feces and uneaten food pellets can escape fish farms and settle onto nearby coral reefs, resulting in algae cover that saps oxygen and blocks light. The Israeli government shut down a fish farm in the Gulf of Eilat in the Red Sea after they discovered catastrophic damage to the nearby coral reef.[124] (The reef has been steadily improving ever since, although oil spills are complicating the improvement.)

Air pollution is not our only crappy concern here. As we have seen in previous chapters, a massive amount of water is needed to keep mega-factories clean. In fact, the majority of water used in factory farms does not go toward hydrating animals. It's used to clean and process animals during slaughter.[125] Once water is used in the industrial farming system, it becomes polluted with animal waste, and it is so teeming with antibiotics, hormones, and bacteria that it cannot be returned to the water system.

This polluted wastewater ends up being stored in massive open-air lagoons that are prone to leaks.[126] Some farmers also routinely drain their cesspools by spraying the waste onto neighboring lands. However, it is not uncommon that a factory farm will produce more waste than can be absorbed into the soil surrounding the facility, and this excess of excrement is often over-applied to fields.[127] Between these two factors, there is an extremely high likelihood that factory farm waste will leak from the lagoons or runoff from the land and enter local water supplies.

What we end up with are dead zones, or areas where hypoxia (decreased levels of oxygen in water) takes place.[128] Dead zones can fluctuate in size with the seasons and move with the tides, but their presence is essentially guaranteed in areas where excess nutrients from conventional industrial

In the U.S., livestock produce 130 times **more waste than humans.**[129] **All this waste contributes to air and water pollution as well as public health concerns.**

agricultural operations enter waterways. Dead zones are created because the excess nitrogen and phosphorus from manure causes massive algae blooms that suck up all the water's oxygen, killing all other plants and marine animals.[130] Algae blooms are responsible for mass fish deaths across the country—some 170,750 miles of river in the U.S. have been deemed impaired due to agricultural runoff.[131]

Across the world, vast areas of oceans and lakes are running out of oxygen, making it nearly impossible for marine life to survive. In the 1960s, 49 dead zones were found in the world's oceans.[132] Today there are more than 400, affecting a total area of 95,000 square miles, which is roughly the size of New Zealand. The largest U.S. dead zone is located at the mouth of the Mississippi River and spans over 8,500 square miles, an area the size of New Jersey.[133]

The world's biggest dead zones are concentrated along the coasts of the U.S., Europe, and China[134]—all places with very high levels of industrial and agricultural runoff.

As the human population continues to grow, so will the need to scale up intensive farming operations. With more animals being killed to meet the escalating demand for meat, dairy, and eggs, we'll be overrun by livestock waste that will far outstrip our ability to develop solutions to manage it safely.

The increased spread of harmful gases, chemicals, toxins, bacteria, and viruses in our air and water will have catastrophic consequences for human health. People living close to farming operations will be hit the worst, but the effects will be felt far and wide.

In the short-term, people will experience eye, nose, mouth, and throat irritations, headaches, and dizziness. Coughing, wheezing, chest tightness, and shortness of breath will become a common part of everyday life as millions of people grapple with the symptoms of asthma and other respiratory illnesses like bronchitis. Prolonged exposure to toxins in the air will lead to long-term effects beyond people's respiratory systems and may lead to immune, neurological, reproductive, and cardiovascular problems, as well as allergies, birth defects, cancer, and, ultimately, death. Our water and food supply will not be free of pathogen contamination and will lead to the rise of skin, stomach, neurological, and reproductive problems as well as the spread of infectious diseases like typhoid, cholera, hepatitis, and malaria.

High antibiotic use in factory farms will lead to an increase in antibiotic-resistant bacteria, known as superbugs, which will be released into the environment via animal waste, causing widespread infections across large sections of the human population. By 2050, 10 million people will die each year as a result of such infections.[135] Disease will be widespread and unrelenting, and the growth and complexity of bacteria strains will far outpace our health care industry's ability to combat them. *totally agree*

If all of this isn't bad enough, the massive amounts of factory farm waste will pollute our streams, rivers, and the oceans, leading to a rise in ocean dead zones, killing millions of marine animals already devastated by overfishing, ocean acidification, and plastic pollution. The oceans regulate our global climate, feed millions of people every year, and produce most of the oxygen we breathe.

As Captain Paul Watson, the founder of the marine conservation organization Sea Shepherd, says, "If the ocean dies, we all die."[136]

If we choose more plant-based foods instead of industrial meat, eggs, and dairy, we automatically reduce the need for industrial farming—and consequently the massive amount of excrement that pollutes our air and water. A meaningful shift away from this industry would have a profound, positive impact on our water and food supply resulting from a reduction in contamination. In turn, this would help prevent the spread of infectious, life-threatening diseases that have the potential to wipe out entire populations of humans and animals.

In addition, by cutting down the massive flow of factory farm pollution currently decimating our rivers and lakes and giving rise to ocean dead zones, we would help repair our failing ocean ecosystems and help them to continue to play their crucial role in sustaining all life on planet Earth.

- Actually really compelling chapter. Makes a lot of good points that don't have easy solutions

- Not a fan of the "all or nothing" approach he takes to the problem. Many things can be done short term to help.

Seven Plants that You Can Grow from Seed to Table in under Two Months

Looking to do more than just eat plants? Perhaps you want to grow them as well? It's more fun than buying food at the supermarket, and it's a lot cheaper.

1. Arugula
A spicy green that can be eaten raw, sautéed, or steamed. It sprouts up so quickly that its nickname is "rocket." Like other leafy greens, arugula requires rich soil and about a foot of growing space. In just over a month you can start harvesting the outer leaves.

2. Bok Choy
Also known as Chinese cabbage, bok choy is a cool-weather vegetable that takes around a week to germinate (i.e., grow from seed to sprout), but it works quickly from then on. Within 45 days, you can start harvesting it for soups, salads, and stir-fries. Bok choy dislikes heat, so plant it in early spring or autumn.

3. Broccoli Rabe
Broccoli rabe is not really broccoli but part of the mustard family. It's quick-growing, and some varieties such as Quarantina mature in just forty days. Broccoli rabe is a cool-weather crop, but some growers say that careful harvesting can keep the crop sprouting through the summer.

4. Cress
This veggie is so easy to grow that no soil is necessary. Many of us have grown cress as sprouts on the windowsill by putting the seeds on a wet paper towel. When the sprouts are a couple of inches high, they can be eaten. For a more significant cress, however, sprinkle the seeds into moist potting soil and let them grow beyond sprouts.

5. Mesclun Mix
Mesclun mix is a combination of loose-leaf lettuces that make great-tasting salads, and they all grow quickly. They need only be distributed in a wide, shallow pot atop a good potting mix and watered well. Harvest the outer leaves and let the plants keep growing.

6. Mustard Greens
Mustard is much more than the familiar yellow condiment. These greens are peppery and are packed with nutrients. They also grow extremely quickly. They like cool weather, wet soil, and frequent harvesting, which should happen when the leaves are 3 to 4 inches long.

7. Radishes
Radishes are a remarkably quick-growing vegetable that add crispness to salads. But don't ignore the radish greens, which can be served in many ways, from stir-fries to soups.

Chapter Six

YOU CAN'T SEE THE FOREST ... OR THE TREES

ISSUES OF DEFORESTATION

Although the world's rainforests cover only around 6 percent of the Earth's land surface, they are home to more than 50 percent of the plants and animals on the planet. These rich and wild forests house iconic species such as toucans, bonobos, jaguars, and sloths. But over the past 40-odd years, a new species, the food grown to feed humans, has managed to make the rainforests home.

Yes, we're talking about cows.

Worldwide, 7 football fields of land are bulldozed every minute to create room for livestock.[137]

Every minute

7 football fields

Every hour

420 football fields

Every day

10,080 football fields

Deforestation accounts for about 10% of all human-induced greenhouse gas emissions.[138]

The world's largest unbroken stretch of tropical rainforest is located in the Amazon River basin in South America and contains one of its most diverse ecosystems. As mentioned in Chapter 1, the Amazon rainforest acts as a vast carbon vacuum that sucks up around 20 percent of greenhouse gases emitted by the burning of fossil fuels, and thereby regulates the planet's climate through the sequestration and storage of carbon dioxide.[139]

In the past 40 years, almost 20 percent of the Amazon rainforest has been destroyed, with more trees being cut down than in the 450 years following the start of European colonization.[140] In the Brazilian region of the Amazon, 80 million cattle roam on land that was once untouched rainforest.[141] In this region, around 80 percent of deforestation is caused by cattle ranching.[142] The losses in this area account for about 14 percent of the world's total annual deforestation, making cattle ranching in the Amazon the largest single driver of deforestation.[143] To put that in even more context, almost 9.9 million acres of forests are destroyed every year and 2.6 million of them are in Brazil alone.[144]

Now, it's not entirely fair to put this all on the cows; in fact, soy production for livestock feed is largely to blame. Brazil has rapidly emerged as one of the largest producers and exporters of beef, poultry, and pork in the world, and the world's largest producer of soybeans.[145] Unfortunately, its rainforests have had to pay the price. Deforestation, much of which is caused by the expansion of soy plantations, accounts for about 15 percent of all human-caused greenhouse gas emissions.[146] Destruction of the rainforests releases the immense amounts of carbon that are stored within trees.

If this keeps up, at some point we won't have any rain-forests to speak of in the next century.

Dear Hiring Manager,

I am reapplying for the position of the Heart and Lungs of planet Earth based on the recommendation of future generations of humans who stand to suffer if I fail to secure this role. I am very interested in this opportunity and believe that my qualifications, education, and professional experience make me a strong candidate.

I believe I am ideally suited for the role you are looking to fill. As a carbon absorption and storage professional, my skills and experience have been well demonstrated during the 400 million years I have existed on this planet. I can promise you that I am uniquely qualified to combat the rising carbon dioxide levels in the Earth's atmosphere by regulating the world's climate and preventing major catastrophic consequences of severe climate change.

My résumé fully details my background and work experience, and how they relate to your needs. As you can see, I have played several important ancillary roles that have benefitted plant and animal species on this planet (including humans) by helping to maintain the world's water cycles, releasing oxygen into the atmosphere, helping to provide crucial medicines, minimizing flooding and soil erosion, providing a habitat for thousands of unique species, and growing a wide range of edible fruits and vegetables enjoyed by humans around the world.

I firmly believe that I can be a valuable asset to your team, and I welcome the opportunity to speak with you about how my experience could help planet Earth achieve its goals of sustaining human life. It is also my firm belief that I am the only qualified applicant for this position.

Thank you in advance for your consideration.

Kind regards,

The World's Tropical Rainforests

Nine Fruits You Should Consider Adding to Your Diet

A plant-based diet offers you opportunities to try all kinds of delicious, nutritious fruits that most Americans have never heard of.

1. Cherimoya

This is a heart-shaped fruit native to South America. It's nicknamed "custard apple" because that's what it tastes like. Mark Twain called it "the most delicious fruit known to men." Other people have compared the taste to bubble gum. An excellent source of vitamin B_6 and a good source of vitamin C and fiber.

2. Atemoya

If you like the cherimoya, then you might also like the atemoya—a hybrid of the cherimoya with the sugar apple (a fruit resembling the raspberry that is native to the Americas). First developed in Miami, Florida, but popular around the world, it tastes like a cherimoya mixed with pineapple and coconut. Low in calories and a good source of vitamin C.

3. Pomelo

Native to South Asia, the pomelo is a citrus fruit that resembles a large pale green grapefruit but is much sweeter tasting. Often used in salads and drinks, it is an excellent source of dietary fiber as well as vitamin C and potassium.

4. Jabuticaba

This Brazilian berry looks like a plum and tastes like a grape. Oddly, it grows on the trunk and branches of its tree rather than on a vine. Because of its short shelf life, it is hard to find far from its Latin American home, but jabuticaba jams and wines are worth seeking out. The fruit is unusually high in protein and calcium.

5. Kiwano Melon

Resembling a spiky alien pod (it was once featured on an episode of *Star Trek: Deep Space Nine*), this fruit is native to South Africa but is now also grown in New Zealand, where it picked up its name due to its resemblance to kiwis. Nicknamed the "horned melon," kiwano melon tastes like a citrusy banana and is loaded with antioxidants, alpha-tocopherol, and vitamin A.

_____

6. Ugli Fruit

Grown primarily in Jamaica, this fruit gained its name due to its remarkably unattractive exterior, but inside the fruit has a refreshing citrusy taste, something like a grapefruit mixed with oranges and tangerines—which, since it was created by hybridizing those fruits, makes sense. Low in calories, it is high in vitamin C and other nutrients.

_____

7. Dragon Fruit

Looking as though someone painted a tennis ball with pink nail polish and added luminescent green tips, dragon fruit, from Central and South America, tastes like a pear and is a good source of vitamin C, while its edible seeds contain omega-3 fatty acids. Loaded with phytonutrients, it is also a natural remedy for constipation.

_____

8. Durian

Called the "King of Fruits," famous (or infamous) for its remarkable stench, resembling a huge green cocklebur, this fruit is commonly found in South Asia. If you're willing to get past the smell, you will be rewarded with a fruit that tastes like a custardy blend of banana and vanilla, with a hint of almonds. Durian is rich in dietary fiber, and an excellent source of B-vitamins, as well as manganese, copper, iron, and magnesium.

_____

9. Pawpaw

Native to North America, and sometimes called a "Kentucky apple," pawpaw is a green fruit with yellowish-orange flesh, and tastes like a banana mixed with a pineapple and mango. Very nutritious, pawpaws are high in vitamin C, potassium, magnesium, and iron, among many other nutrients. The name probably derives from the Spanish papaya, which the fruit vaguely resembles.

_____

The loss of our rainforests would also mean the loss of millions of plant and animal species, and as the dominoes of extinction set off by this loss begin to fall, they very well might end with us. The Amazon, for example, currently produces up to 25 percent of the plants used in modern medicines.[147] The rainforests are also home to fruits and vegetables that make up a large portion of the global agricultural supply. Loss of the rainforests' diverse animal species also means the loss of the ecosystem services they provide, such as pollination, maintenance of soil structure and fertility, as well as nutrient cycling.

Losing the rainforests would also mean losing one of our biggest sources of freshwater. Rainforests play a crucial role in moderating weather and precipitation cycles by releasing moisture into the atmosphere. Without them, rainfall patterns are likely to be significantly altered globally. This would lead to drought-like conditions across the planet and severe water shortages in the regions around the rainforests that have become dependent on water from them for their economic activity.

Lastly, the loss of rainforests would significantly speed up climate change because of the decreased number of trees combatting the rising greenhouse gas emissions. The result would be an acceleration in the rise of global temperatures, coupled with floods, famine, disease, war, and global economic unrest.

If we shift our diet away from one dominated by industrial animal-based foods, we can significantly slow down the rate of rainforest destruction. The positive impact would be huge. First, the millions of species that call the rainforests home would be spared the devastating losses of their natural habitats.

Humans would stand to benefit as well. Billions of people who rely on the rainforest either directly or indirectly for everything from freshwater to fruits, nuts, and medicine, would be given a fighting chance of survival and the chance to find new, constructive, and sustainable uses for this land as we prepare for the population to grow to 9.8 billion by the year 2050.

Rainforests are one of our best allies in the fights against climate change and species extinction. Together, we could help protect them by doing little more than rethinking what we eat.

Chapter Seven

THE SILENCE OF THE LAMBS ... AND THE LIONS ... AND THE BIRDS ... AND THE FISH ...

ISSUES OF SPECIES EXTINCTION

The world is currently experiencing the sixth mass extinction[148] event in its history, involving the highest rate of species die-off since the loss of dinosaurs 65 million years ago.

Since 1970, there has already been a 58 percent overall decline in the numbers of fish, mammals, birds, and reptiles worldwide.[149] Species are becoming extinct as much as 1,000 times more frequently now than in the 60 million years before people came along.[150] While the other five extinction events were caused by natural disasters, this one is on us.

We are driving this sixth extinction event in four ways.

First, the increasing globalization of human trade and agriculture led to the introduction of invasive species (flora and fauna) that compete within the native ecosystem, causing food and water scarcities that result in extinction.

Second, we have become the top predator on land and at sea, consuming 20 to 40 percent of the planet's animals. We are killing off species with a combination of overexploitation and ecosystem changes.

Third, humanity has become a massive force in directing evolution not only via domestication of animals and cultivation of crops, but also by using molecular techniques to manipulate genomes.

Fourth, the technology we have created has begun to act practically independently, thereby creating what scientists refer to as the "technosphere."[151] The concept of the technosphere, pioneered by Peter Haff of Duke University, refers to the sum total of all human-made manufactured machines and objects, and the systems that control them.

Up to 137 plant, animal, and insect species are lost every day due to rainforest destruction.

According to Haff, technology—from stone tools, wheels, and crops to current technology—has already acted independently to create a new sphere that can be compared to the existing biosphere or atmosphere or lithosphere. The domestication of animals and the industrialization of farming along with its discarded waste and pollution are part of this technosphere. We created these systems and objects and beings to keep us alive, and consequently we have lost control over the downstream dynamics and energy flows of these systems we rely upon. This technosphere now weighs 30 trillion tons[152] and, when compared with the biosphere, is remarkably poor at recycling its own materials, thereby causing significant damage to plant and animal species on the planet. For example, there are more than 5 trillion pieces of plastic in the world's oceans and 700 different marine species are in danger of extinction due to the threat of ingestion, entanglement, and pollution.[153]

The rise of factory farming as the leading means of feeding our planet's population is one great example of how all four of the factors driving this extinction event have come together. Sadly, the convergence of these factors has wreaked havoc on the planet's ecosystems and pushed thousands of species to the brink of extinction. This is because livestock (and the crops that feed them) take up space . . . a LOT of space. Many of these animals are not native to their new homes;[154] they were brought there by humans. So, for these animals to be on this land, something else needed to go.

Sixty percent[155] of global biodiversity loss results from meat-based diets, which puts a huge strain on the Earth's resources. More than 175 species[156] are threatened, endangered, or imperiled by livestock on federal lands in the United States alone. From wolves to elk to prairie dogs, wild animals pay the price of meat production. Some are killed because they prey on cows. Others die en masse to make room for agricultural operations—and still more are put in harm's way by pollution and greenhouse gas emissions that exacerbate climate change.

To protect lands designated for cattle grazing, the American wild horse has been subject to brutal round-ups[157] that kill and maim members of dwindling herds. When even one species disappears, biodiversity drops and the fundamental functions of native ecosystems[158] are altered.

Wolves and other predators perceived as a danger to livestock[159] are constantly under threat within the United States and are being targeted in an extermination campaign sponsored by the U.S. Fish and Wildlife Service.[160] The Mexican gray wolf has already become extinct in Southwestern ecosystems due to "predator control" systems crafted to protect livestock.[161]

The threat beef production poses to wildlife also extends to the tropics,[162] where deforestation is putting animals such as jaguars on the brink of extinction.[163] As deforestation drives the destruction of jaguar habitat, it also destroys the habitat of its natural prey, leading jaguars to atypically prey on domestic cattle. This means that jaguars are dually threatened by deforestation itself and by direct hunting when they imperil the bottom line of cattle interests.

These are just some of the many species directly impacted by widespread deforestation and habitat destruction caused by our current industrialized food system.

In addition, rising temperatures and changing weather and vegetation patterns across the planet are forcing animals to migrate to new, cooler areas for survival. However, because of the rapid nature of climate change, many species will not be able to migrate or adjust in time. If climate change continues on its current track, one out of every six species on Earth could be at risk of extinction.[164]

The danger is by no means limited to land. As explained in Chapter 6, factory farm runoff eventually makes its way into the oceans, causing massive dead zones. Further, as sea temperatures rise, the oceans become increasingly acidic (through absorption of carbon dioxide), harming marine animals and coral reefs. Add to it the proliferation of large-scale commercial fishing operations, and you have a perfect storm that pushes many species of fish to the brink of extinction.

If you thought seafood was not part of the equation of environmental destruction caused by your food choices, you'd be mistaken. In just 55 years, humans have managed to wipe out 90 percent of the ocean's top predators.[165] The depletion of these species causes a shift in the ecosystems of entire oceans where commercially valuable fish are replaced by smaller, plankton-feeding fish. If we keep fishing at our current rate, all species of wild seafood will collapse within 50 years.[166]

Massive swaths of coral reefs are already suffering irreversible damage because of ocean acidification, bleaching, and destructive fishing techniques such as bottom trawling, which literally crushes deep-sea coral with weighted nets.[167] Corals host the most biodiverse ecosystems in the world, and reefs are often referred to as "Rainforests of the Ocean." Much like their terrestrial counterparts, underwater rainforests are extraordinarily useful. In total, coral reefs cover about 0.1 percent of the world's oceans, but they nurture 25 percent of its marine species. If these marine species are lost, the impact would be devastating for around 500 million people who depend on coral eco-systems to support their livelihood.[168] In many ways, coral reefs are the ocean's lifelines. Their disappearance could create an ecologically devastating domino effect for all life on Earth.

Just 2% of wild bee
species contribute 80%
of the crop pollination
observed globally.

A meteor might have killed the dinosaurs, but the next mass extinction will be on us. By the year 2050, one-fourth of the world's plant and vertebrate animal species could face extinction.[169] Extinction matters, because with each species lost, diversity diminishes along with the complexity of ecosystems that make up life on Earth. From the top to the bottom of the food chain, there are many plant and animal species that are crucial to the existence of their ecosystems as we know them. Even one species disappearing may have colossal downstream implications on other plant and animal species, ultimately affecting humans.

As one example, accelerating rates of climate change driven by our reliance on the industrial livestock system will cause changes in temperature, causing flowers to bloom earlier, which will leave bees unable to adapt quickly enough and pollinate in time.[170] As a result, bees will struggle to obtain nectar for their hives, resulting in a decline in bee populations. The decline of bees alone will lead to massive disruption in our food system, as bees are responsible for pollinating approximately 250,000 plant species[171] that are crucial for the survival of not just other animals, but humans as well. Just 2 percent of wild bee species contribute 80 percent of the crop pollination observed globally.[172] This means that if this small percentage of bee species disappears, then 80 percent of our agricultural system could collapse, further exacerbating the global hunger crisis and the global wars that follow.

Nine Great Animals That No Longer Exist

1. Auroch

When you look at a cow today, you are looking at a descendant of what was once a common type of cattle that roamed Europe, Asia, and North Africa. The last recorded auroch died in Poland, in 1627. Aurochs were domesticated by humans about 10,000 years ago, but died from overhunting, the narrowing of their habitat due to farming, and possibly diseases transmitted from other animals. (There are, however, efforts to bring the Auroch back in Europe.[173])

2. California Grizzly (Golden) Bear

A subspecies of the grizzly bear, this large creature once roamed from Alaska to California, eventually becoming the symbol pictured on the California state flag. It is also the mascot of the Universities of California in Berkeley, Los Angeles, and Riverside. That didn't stop Californians from killing every one of them. The last one was shot in 1922. The golden grizzly has been recently posited for de-extinction through genetic engineering or other laboratory processes.

3. Dodo

One of the most famous of the extinct animals, the dodo, a flightless bird, was about 3 feet tall and weighed up to 40 pounds. The dodo, whose population may have already been dwindling, first encountered humans around 1600 on its native island of Mauritius in the Indian Ocean, and was extinct within seven decades, mostly because the dodo had no fear of humans, which made it easy prey for hunters.

4. Great Auk

Another flightless bird, the great auk became extinct in the mid-nineteenth century. Thirty inches tall and about 10 pounds, with a black back and a white belly, it vaguely resembled a penguin, and was, in fact, the first bird to be called one, although it turned out not to be related to penguins. It was particularly valued for its down, which probably helped lead to its extinction. The last two great auks were killed off of Iceland in 1844.

5. Laughing Owl

The laughing owl, which went extinct by the beginning of World War I, had a call that was described as "a loud cry made up of a series of dismal shrieks frequently repeated." Found in New Zealand, it was widely and easily hunted, which probably caused its extinction. The bird should not be confused with the dozens of videos on YouTube of owls that are laughing.

6. Passenger Pigeon

This poor pigeon, whose name comes from the French *passager*, as in "passing by," as opposed to a pigeon who carried passengers, was a small brown bird found in eastern America. At one point its population reached about 5 billion. However it was easily shot and therefore its meat was cheap. Additionally, its habitat shrank as humans deforested the countryside. Due to these factors, it was extinct by the beginning of the twentieth century. The last known passenger pigeon, named Martha, died at the Cincinnati Zoo in 1914.

7. Quagga

The quagga was a member of the zebra family and lived in South Africa until the end of the nineteenth century. About 8 feet long and 4½ feet tall, the quagga was hunted to extinction, the last one dying in captivity in 1883. In 1984 the quagga was the first extinct animal whose DNA was analyzed, and a group of South Africans are trying to resurrect the species through selective breeding with extant zebras. Several foals have been produced that resemble the striping pattern of the quagga, including one named Henry and one named Freddy.

8. Tasmanian Tiger

A shy, nocturnal marsupial whose family members have been around for tens of millions of years, this doglike creature, related to the Tasmanian devil, was already becoming rare in Australia before hunters helped kill it off by the 1930s, with the aid of a dwindling habitat taken over by humans. This is one extinct animal, however, that people sometimes claim they still see. Media mogul Ted Turner once offered $100,000 to anyone who could prove its existence. No one did.

9. Woolly Mammoth

The woolly mammoth thrived in the Pleistocene era, which lasted from about 2,588,000 to 11,700 years ago. A distant relative of the Asian elephant, we know a great deal about this animal because it was so often depicted in cave paintings, and also because many of its skeletons and carcasses have been discovered in frozen environments. Its disappearance was most likely caused by a combination of climate change, a shrinking of habitat, and human hunting.

But the collapse of the bees will be just one among several triggers that will eventually lead to devastation on a global scale. As species across the Earth's land and oceans start to succumb to the effects of habitat loss, pollution, and a warming climate, the balance of the ecosystems they inhabit will be thrown off completely. Once one species falls, like dominoes, the other species (whether predator or prey) in its food chain will eventually collapse.

Now imagine this happening at an accelerated pace, all across the globe. The end result will be a destruction of the natural balance as we know it, threatening the survival of none other than the species that sits at the apex of the food chain . . . humans.

If we choose more plant-based foods and shift away from our meat-heavy diets, we can drastically cut down our greenhouse gas emissions, slow down habitat destruction, and thereby give thousands of species a fighting chance of survival. This will prevent the devastating consequence of accelerated loss of key species that hold together the delicate fabric that makes up the complex web of life on planet Earth.

We are, after all, not independent of this web, but a key part of it, and by helping to slow down the pace of extinction of other species, we are helping none more than our own.

Chapter Eight

THE #EATFOR THE PLANET WAY

A BETTER PATH

If you haven't figured this out by now, the future of our planet and our species appears to be pretty bleak. If current trends continue, we face a high risk of catastrophic climate change and environmental destruction, causing drought, flood, famine, mass species extinction, war, disease, and ultimately economic and ecosystem collapse.

The good news?

We still have a fighting chance.

But in order for us to course-correct in time for meaningful change to unfold, we have to kick-start a global sustainable food movement right now. Business as usual is not going to cut it any longer. It's time for each and every one of us to recognize that the industrial livestock system is at the heart of our environmental crisis.

The best part is that we can all exercise our individual power to be a part of the solution starting today. After all, the real battle for the future of our planet—and the future of the human race—is being fought on our plates, multiple times a day, with every food choice we make.

So is it as simple as turning our backs on meat, dairy, eggs, and seafood?

The answer is yes, and no. Because, as simple as this solution may seem, here's where things have the potential to get fairly complicated. Changing food habits is diffcult and personal. For most of us, our food and cooking habits represent a lot more than simply the means by which we consume calories to stay alive.

Food plays a role in every culture and personal identity that far exceeds the purpose of nourishing our bodies. As author Jonathan Safran Foer put it, "Food is not rational. Food is culture, habit, craving, and identity." That's because food is life and the type of ingredients used, methods of preparation, flavors, and presentation techniques come to define who we are as people. You are what you eat in more ways than one, and you now have the power to become a world-changer by changing what's on your plate.

And if you pay close attention to the three-step framework outlined here, you'll come to realize that it's never been easier.

It starts here. Think you can't give up on bacon and steak? Fair enough, but do you still want to make your meat-eating sustainable? The answer isn't simply grass-fed or pasture-raised beef, organic milk, and free-range eggs. The only sustainable way for large populations of people to eat animal products is to eat much less of them. Just cutting back on your consumption of these foods gives you the potential to make a tremendous, positive impact on the health of the planet (as well as your health).

Start by leaving these foods off your plate even just one day a week, or one meal a day. Or, try limiting consumption of your meaty favorites to just the weekend. Another idea: Think of animal foods as a luxury, rather than a necessity, and try to eliminate them from your home cooking except, perhaps, for special gatherings. Or, you can try reserving them for occasions when you are dining out in a group. Even a nominal effort to cut back will go a long way in helping to make a dent in the demand for these environmentally destructive foods. One small step for your diet, one large step for the planet.

The best part is you get to decide how and when you choose to implement this step.

Here's where things start to get interesting, and your efforts to moderate your consumption of animal foods feel less like you're depriving yourself and more like you're redefining your understanding of your favorite foods.

Driven by increasing consumer demand for healthier, cleaner protein sources, over the last few years the food industry has been undergoing a significant shift. Companies are starting to use new practices in science and technology to introduce innovative products in the market that are better for us and for the planet than the foods they are replacing. Food scientists are busy breaking down the structural components of meat and other animal sources of protein, turning to the plant kingdom, and using computing power to find viable replicas or combinations that can result in a product that tastes, feels, and even smells like the real thing with an identical (or, most often, enhanced) nutritional profile.

The days where you would only find the label "vegan" or "plant-based" on one or two frozen soy burgers at the grocery store are long gone. In the past few years, a mix of established natural food brands and innovative new start-ups have completely changed the game by offering everything from delicious artisan nut-based cheeses to mouthwatering beef-less burgers (some that even bleed like their animal-based counterparts)[174] and other meat alternatives, as well as a plethora of dairy-free milks, snacks, and much more—all foods that pack the same amount (or more) of flavor and nutrition as their animal-based counterparts.

A simple step to take: Examine packaged food products you would normally place in your grocery cart and look for plant-based alternatives. Milk, butter, mayo, cheese, grilled chicken, ground beef, sausages, cold cuts, etc., are all great places to test out plant-based alternatives that are becoming healthier, tastier, and consequently more popular by the day. In some categories, such as milk, the plant-based alternatives like almond milk are challenging their animal-based competitors.

By replacing your favorite animal-based staples with sustainable options like plant-based meats, milks, and cheeses, you will automatically be making a daily food choice that uses significantly fewer resources. According to a study of the environmental impacts of 39 meat substitutes presented at the American Society for Nutrition Annual Meeting in April 2016, plant-based meat alternatives were found to be associated with substantially lower emissions than actual meat. Specifically, these alternatives were associated with ten times less greenhouse gas emissions than producing comparable beef-based products.[175] That's a significant difference.

So start swapping out those staples in your grocery cart and help to support a whole new category of plant-based foods that have the power to shape our global food system into a more sustainable and just one.

Eight Excellent Substitutes for Meat

If you're looking to create your own plant-based dinners at home, the following are some of the more popular meat substitutes on the market.

1. Tofu

Originally created in China more than 2,000 years ago, tofu is made by curdling soymilk. Tofu comes in several textures (silken to extra firm) and can be fried, grilled, baked, and shaped into meat-like products. Though bland on its own, seasoned tofu quickly absorbs the flavors of other ingredients.

2. Tempeh

Like tofu, tempeh is made from soybeans, except that tempeh is fermented, which many experts believe gives it a nutritional advantage over tofu.

3. Portobello Mushrooms

Already on the menu in many vegetarian restaurants as substitute burgers, these juicy mushrooms are relatively high in protein and resemble meat more than any other vegetable. Shiitake mushrooms can also make a reasonable meat substitute.

4. Seitan

Pronounced "say-tan," this is also known as "wheat meat." It originated in Japan about 1,000 years ago. Prepared from wheat gluten, seitan soaks up the flavor of whatever sauce it is prepared in, so it can be used as an excellent substitute for more delicate meats such as veal.

5. Legumes

Lentils, peas, and beans are also already on many burger menus, as their color and texture lend themselves to being pressed into hamburger-lookalike patties.

6. Textured Vegetable Protein (TVP)

Made from soy flour and generally sold in bags of breadcrumb-like pieces, TVP was invented by food processing and commodities trading conglomerate Archer Daniels Midland in the 1960s. Bland-tasting TVP absorbs the flavors of the ingredients with which it is mixed.

7. Jackfruit

Native to southeast Asia, jackfruit is the only fruit that can reliably substitute for meat. It works best with sauces and is often prepared to resemble pulled pork.

8. Nuts

Nuts are frequently added to plant-burgers to enhance texture and taste, but can also be used on their own as a meat substitute.

There's a whole wide world of food out there about which most people know little or nothing. The more you explore the possibilities of plant-based food, the more you'll realize that you can broaden your food choices by discovering new cuisines, fresh ingredients, and endless creative ways that vegetables and other plant-based foods can be cooked, grilled, baked, and sautéed in your home kitchen. It's not about giving up foods you love; it's about enjoying the process of discovering new ones, as well as recreating old favorites without the unnecessary negative impacts of animal products.

Keep the following rules in mind when choosing plant-based foods: Try to buy produce, grains, nuts, and seeds that are locally grown. Not only are such foods fresh, but they have not been air-freighted or hauled across the country to reach your grocery cart. To ensure that your produce is local, shop at a farmers' market or look for identifying stickers in your grocery store.

Also, when possible, choose organic so that you can avoid produce that's been sprayed with environmentally harmful pesticides (these are hardly good for your health, either). However, in a pinch, it's probably better to buy local, non-organic produce instead of organic items that have been shipped very far distances. It is also helpful to buy produce that is in season, and if available, look for foods that are grown using regenerative agriculture methods. Garden peas, lentils, beans, broccoli, tomatoes, and potatoes all use comparatively less resources and are responsible for far less greenhouse gas emissions.

Your parents were right when they told you to eat your vegetables, but long gone are the days when mashed potatoes or boiled spinach are the only veggie options available. Plant-based cooking has radically transformed over the past few years. The depth and breadth of possibilities when it comes to cooking without meat, dairy, eggs, or seafood are virtually limitless. You can now make hearty burgers, decadent desserts, and all your other favorite foods using a handful of simple, plant-based ingredients that are available in many major grocery stores. It's no coincidence that so many notable food trends in recent years, like clean eating, have been centered around plant-based foods.

So, shift vegetables, grains, and plant proteins like lentils, nuts, seeds, and beans to the center of your plate, and shove meat, dairy, eggs, and seafood to the side—or better yet, off of it altogether!

It's time we stepped off the path on which we've been traveling, driven by our industrialized food system and dominated by animal agriculture. At the end of that road is a future where not only is the natural beauty and diversity of the Earth completely devastated, but so is any hope for a healthy and thriving human population. Is this the future you envision for your children and their children?

We currently stand at the precipice of what might seem like impending doom, but each and every one of us has the key to help neutralize the threat. It's a moment where we can choose to take control of, or be a victim of, a food system that is leading us down the wrong path. When all is said and done, do you want to be remembered as someone who could have made a difference but didn't because of habit, cultural conditioning, or apathy? You owe it to yourself and future generations to give it a try.

Food is complicated—it represents culture, comfort, and family. It has deeply personal meanings to all of us. And in the stressful modern world, where our senses are constantly overstimulated, the food choices we make often tend to be impulsive, irrational, and counterintuitive.

The best part of the #EatForThePlanet way is that it's not about restricting your diet but about changing the way you think about your food choices and keeping up with the changing times. It's not about giving up foods as much as discovering new, healthier, and more interesting options.

Start anywhere, but start today. Go as far as you are willing to take yourself, but get on the right path. Make the decision to reduce your impact on the world around you. Think about it: Perhaps you already recycle, use a reusable grocery bag, ride a bicycle to work, carpool, eat locally, or carry a water bottle. It's time to start thinking of your food as another excellent way to make our planet beautiful and safe for our children and their children. It's time to eat in a way that nourishes you without starving the planet.

Eat intelligently. Eat well. Eat for the planet.

Twelve Books to Read on Other Issues Concerning Our Environment and Our Future

1. *The Beekeeper's Lament: How One Man and Half a Billion Honey Bees Help Feed America*, by Hannah Nordhaus (2011). An award-winning journalist describes the importance of honeybees to our world, and in doing so, provides a gripping story of the relationship between one particular species and our entire food chain.

2. *Cadillac Desert: The American West and Its Disappearing Water*, by Marc Reisner (1986). A wonderfully written exposé of how the American West was settled without regard to the land's ecology. An updated edition was published in 1993, and a four-part documentary appeared on PBS in 1997.

3. *Cradle to Cradle: Remaking the Way We Make Things*, by Michael Braungart and William McDonough (2002). A controversial examination of how humans create and manufacture products, proposing that we look to nature for our role model and manufacture items that impact the world in a positive way long after the product's preliminary use has been discarded.

4. *Eaarth: Making a Life on a Tough New Planet*, by Bill McKibben (2010). Written by one of the first people to warn about climate change, this book is a powerful and compelling argument as to how humans must change our ways to save our planet.

5. *Half-Earth*, by Edward O. Wilson (2016). Besides being one of the world's most important scientists and a two-time Pulitzer Prize winner, biologist Wilson is also an excellent writer; his latest book argues that the dire situation facing us needs a grand solution—dedicate half of the Earth's surface to nature.

6. *An Inconvenient Truth: The Planetary Emergency of Global Warming and What We Can Do About It*, by Al Gore (2006). This modern classic by the former vice president, based on his wildly popular lecture tours, warns us that if humans don't take action to fight global climate change, the human race, our fellow creatures on Earth, and the Earth itself, are all in peril.

7. *A Sand County Almanac*, by Aldo Leopold (1949). Six decades old, but increasingly relevant with climate change and the need to understand the seasons, this series of essays is considered one of the most influential nature books ever written (along with, of course, Henry David Thoreau's *Walden*, 1854).

8. *Silent Spring*, by Rachel Carson (1962). First published as articles in *The New Yorker*, and in many ways the progenitor of most of the other books on this list, Carson documents the effects of the indiscriminate use of pesticides on the environment, both sparking a new awareness of the way humans treat the Earth and helping to create the 1960s environmental movement.

9. *The Sixth Extinction: An Unnatural History*, by Elizabeth Kolbert (2014). Winner of the Pulitzer Prize, this well-researched and documented book details the events of the Earth's first five mass extinctions, all caused by natural events, and explains why we are in the middle of the sixth one, this one precipitated by humans.

10. *Storms of My Grandchildren: The Truth About the Coming Climate Catastrophe and Our Last Chance to Save Humanity*, by James Hansen (2009). One of the world's foremost climatologists explains what climate change really is, predicts what will happen to the Earth if we don't take action to fight it, and also shows that there is still time to remedy the problem.

11. *This Changes Everything: Capitalism vs. The Climate*, by Naomi Klein (2014). A powerful examination of why we must consider rethinking our basic current economic and political systems in order to save the world—and why we must do so soon.

12. *The World Is Blue: How Our Fate and the Ocean's Are One*, by Sylvia A. Earle (2009). In this tie-in to a *National Geographic* magazine project, Earle clearly and insightfully explains the intricate and critical relationship between our health and the health of our oceans.

Six Documentaries That Explore the Relationship Between Food and Our World

1. *The Cove*, directed by Louie Psihoyos (2009). This beautifully filmed documentary, which won an Oscar as well as twenty-five other film awards, explores the practice of dolphin hunting in Japan, exposing the cruelty of the hunt as well as its other potentially harmful ramifications.

2. *Cowspiracy: The Sustainability Secret*, produced and directed by Kip Anderson and Keegan Kuhn (2014). Crowd-funded on the website Indiegogo, this appealing, well-researched documentary explores the relationship between animal agriculture and the environment.

3. *Earthlings*, directed by Shaun Monson (2005). *Earthlings* tackles the complicated twenty-first-century relationship between humans and animals. According to the film's narrator Joaquin Phoenix, "Of all the films I have ever made, this is the one that gets people talking the most. For every one person who sees *Earthlings*, they will tell three."

4. *Food, Inc.*, directed by Robert Kenner (2008). This Oscar-nominated documentary examines the repercussions of corporate farming in America, showing how agribusiness creates a food system that is harmful to both humans and animals.

5. *The Ghosts in Our Machine*, directed by Liz Marshall (2013). Marshall follows photojournalist Jo-Anne McArthur as she investigates such places as fur farms and animal sanctuaries; Marshall's motivation was "to give a voice to the non-human world." The film does exactly that.

6. *Speciesism: The Movie*, directed by Mark Devries (2013). A fascinating discussion of the way humans treat animals and all the complex issues that topic creates, related in a remarkably nonconfrontational, easy-to-watch style. Its tagline is accurate: "After watching *Speciesism: The Movie*, you'll never look at animals the same way again. Especially humans."

Notes

1   Farm Forward calculation based on U.S. Department of Agriculture, 2002 Census of Agriculture, June 2004; and Environmental Protection Agency, Producers' Compliance Guide for CAFOs, August 2003.

2   "History of Life on Earth." BBC Nature. www.bbc.co.uk/nature/history_of_the_earth.

3   Nierenberg, Danielle. "Chapter 2: Rethinking the Global Meat Industry." Worldwatch Institute. www.worldwatch.org/node/3993.

4   Bourne, Joel K. "Special Report: Cheap Food." *National Geographic* (June 2009). gm.nationalgeographic.com/2009/06/cheap-food/bourne-text.

5   Schecter, Peter, and Jason Marczak. "U.S. Must Act to Prevent Regional Energy Crisis." *CNN Global Public Square* (July 31, 2014). globalpublicsquare.blogs.cnn.com/2014/07/31/u-s-must-act-to-prevent-regional-energy-crisis/.

6   Plumer, Brad. "Where the World's Running out of Water, in One Map." *The Washington Post* (August 10, 2012). www.washingtonpost.com/blogs/wonkblog/wp/2012/08/10/where-the-worlds-running-out-of-water-in-one-map/.

7   Tucker, Jessica. "Meat and Its Impact on the Environment: Should We Blame Farmers or Meat Eaters?" *One Green Planet* (May 2, 2014). www.onegreenplanet.org/animalsandnature/meat-and-the-environment-blame-farmers-or-meat-eaters/.

8   Eshel, G. et al. "Land, Irrigation Water, Greenhouse Gas, and Reactive Nitrogen Burdens of Meat, Eggs, and Dairy Production in the United States." *Proceedings of the National Academy of Sciences of the United States of America*. U.S. National Library of Medicine (August 19. 2014). www.ncbi.nlm.nih.gov/pubmed/25049416.

9   Goodland, Robert and Jeff Anhang. "Livestock and Climate Change." *World Watch*. World Watch Institute (November 2009). www.worldwatch.org/files/pdf/Livestock%20and%20Climate%20Change.pdf.

10 Thornton, Philip et al. "Livestock and Climate Change." International Livestock Research Institute (November 2011). cgspace.cgiar.org/bitstream/handle/10568/10601/IssueBrief3.pdf.

11 European Commission, Joint Research Centre (JRC). "Urbanization: 95% of the World's Population Lives on 10% of the Land." *ScienceDaily* (December 19, 2008). www.sciencedaily.com/releases/2008/12/081217192745.htm.

12 Goodland, Robert and Jeff Anhang. "Livestock and Climate Change." *World Watch*. World Watch Institute (November 2009). www.worldwatch.org/files/pdf/Livestock%20and%20Climate%20Change.pdf.

13 Matthews, Christopher. "Livestock a Major Threat to Environment." Food and Agriculture Organization of the United Nations (November 29, 2006). www.fao.org/Newsroom/en/news/2006/1000448/index.html.

14 Miller, Scot M. et al. "Anthropogenic Emissions of Methane in the United States." *PNAS* 10:50 (December 10, 2013). www.pnas.org/citmgr?gca=pnas%3B110%2F50%2F20018.

15 "World Agriculture: Towards 2015/2030. Summary Report." Food and Agriculture Organization of the United Nations, Economic and Social Development Department. www.fao.org/docrep/004/y3557e/y3557e11.htm.

16 Barry, John Byrne. "Year of the Pig." *Sierra Club: The Planet Newsletter* 5:7 (September 1998). vault.sierraclub.org/planet/199807/beat.asp.

17 "Rearing Cattle Produces More Greenhouse Gases Than Driving Cars, UN Report Warns." UN News Centre (November 20, 2006). www.un.org/apps/news/story.asp?newsID=20772#.WTBf1xPytao.

18 "Nitrous Oxide." BBC Weather Centre. www.bbc.co.uk/climate/evidence/nitrous_oxide.shtml.

19 "Rearing Cattle Produces More Greenhouse Gases Than Driving Cars, UN Report Warns." UN News Centre (November 20, 2006). www.un.org/apps/news/story.asp?newsID=20772#.WTBf1xPytao.

20 Goodland, Robert and Jeff Anhang. "Livestock and Climate Change." *World Watch*. World Watch Institute (November 2009). www.worldwatch.org/files/pdf/Livestock%20and%20Climate%20Change.pdf.

21 "Livestock and Landscapes." FAO (2012). www.fao.org/docrep/018/ar591e/ar591e.pdf.

22 Oswalt, Sonja N. et al. "Forest Resources of the United States, 2012." USDA (October 2014). www.srs.fs.usda.gov/pubs/gtr/gtr_wo091.pdf.

23 Ketler, Alanna. "Factory Farming Is Destroying Our Environment." *Collective Evolution* (August 26, 2013). www.collective-evolution. com/2013/03/04/eating-meat-destruction-of-environment/.

24 Veiga, J. B. et al. "Cattle Ranching in the Amazon Rainforest." FAO, XII World Forestry Congress (2003). www.fao.org/docrep/ ARTICLE/WFC/XII/0568-B1.HTM.

25 Aldridge, Tom and Herb Schlubach. "Water Requirements for Food Production," *Soil and Water* 38 (Fall 1978), University of California Cooperative Extension, 13017; Paul and Anne Ehrlich, *Population, Resources, Environment.* (San Francisco: Freeman, 1972), pp. 75–76.

26 "Facts on Animal Farming and the Environment." *One Green Planet* (December 17, 2014). www.onegreenplanet.org/ animalsandnature/facts-on-animal-farming-and-the-environment/.

27 "World Population Projected to Reach 9.7 Billion by 2050" United Nations, Department of Economic and Social Affairs (July 29, 2015). www.un.org/en/development/desa/news/ population/2015-report.html.

28 Brinkman, Henk-Jan and Cullen S. Hendrix. "Food Insecurity and Violent Conflict: Causes, Consequences, and Addressing the Challenges." World Food Programme (July 2011). documents.wfp.org/stellent/groups/ public/documents/newsroom/wfp238358. pdf?

29 Stehfest, Elke et al. "Climate Benefits of Changing Diet." Springer Science + Business Media (February 2009). doi:10.1007/s10584-008-9534-6.

30 "How Much Water Is There on, in, and above the Earth?" USGS: Science for a Changing World (December 2, 2016). water.usgs.gov/edu/ earthhowmuch.html.

31 "The World's Water." USGS Water Science School. water.usgs.gov/edu/earthwherewater. html.

32 "Freshwater Crisis." *National Geographic*, www.nationalgeographic.com/freshwater/ freshwater-crisis.html.

33 "Livestock's Long Shadow: Environmental Issues and Options." FAO (2006). ftp://ftp.fao. org/docrep/fao/010/a0701e/a0701e04.pdf.

34 "Farm Animal Statistics: Slaughter Totals." The Humane Society of the United States. www.humanesociety.org/news/ resources/research/stats_slaughter_totals. html?referrer=https%3A%2F%2Fwww. google.com%2F.

35 "Below-Cost Feed Crops: An Indirect Subsidy for Industrial Animal Factories." Institute for Agriculture and Trade Policy: Trade and Global Governance Program (June 2006). www.iatp. org/sites/default/files/258_2_88122_0.pdf

36 "The Water Footprint of Food." GRACE Communications Foundation. www.gracelinks. org/1361/the-waterfootprint-of-food.

37 Hallock, Betty. "To Make a Burger, First You Need 660 Gallons of Water . . . " *Los Angeles Times* (January 7, 2014). www.latimes.com/ food/dailydish/la-dd-gallons-of-water-to-make-a-burger-20140124-story.html.

38 "Cattle & Beef: Background" USDA – ERS. www. ers.usda.gov/topics/animal-products/cattle-beef/background.aspx.

39 Mekonnen, M. M. and A. Y. Hoekstra. "The Green, Blue and Grey Water Footprint of Farm Animals and Animal Products." *Value of Water Research Report Series* 48 (December 2010). UNESCO-IHE. waterfootprint.org/ media/downloads/Report-48-WaterFootprint-AnimalProducts-Vol1.pdf.

40 Mekonnen, M. M. and A. Y. Hoekstra. "The Green, Blue and Grey Water Footprint of Farm Animals and Animal Products." *Value of Water Research Report Series* 48 (December 2010). UNESCO-IHE. waterfootprint.org/ media/downloads/Report-48-WaterFootprint-AnimalProducts-Vol1.pdf.

41 "Dairy Facts." University of Arkansas System: Division of Agriculture, Research & Extension. www.uaex.edu/4h-youth/activities-programs/ docs/Dairy%20Facts.pdf.

42 Park, Alex and Julia Lurie. "It Takes HOW Much Water to Make Greek Yogurt?!" *Mother Jones* (June 24, 2017). www.motherjones.com/ environment/2014/03/california-water-suck/.

43 de Ondarza, Mary Beth. "Water." *Back to First Page* (December 29, 2000). www. milkproduction.com/Library/Scientific-articles/Housing/Water/.

44 "Agricultural Waste Management Field Handbook." U.S. Department of Agriculture, Soil Conservation Service (April 1992), pp. 4–8. policy.nrcs.usda.gov/viewerFS. aspx?hid=21430

45 "Is Meat Sustainable?" *World Watch*. Worldwatch Institute (August 2004). www. worldwatch.org/node/549.

46 "Indoor Water Use in the United States." EPA WaterSense (June 2008). www.epa.gov/sites/ production/files/2017-03/documents/ws-facthseet-indoor-water-use-in-the-us.pdf.

47 "The Hidden Water We Use." *National Geographic*, environment.nationalgeographic. com/environment/freshwater/embedded-water/.

48 "Per Capita Consumption of Poultry and Livestock, 1965 to Estimated 2018, in Pounds." The National Chicken Council. www. nationalchickencouncil.org/about-the-industry/ statistics/per-capita-consumption-of-poultry-and-livestock-1965-to-estimated-2012-in-pounds/.

49 "The Hidden Water We Use." *National Geographic*, environment.nationalgeographic. com/environment/freshwater/embedded-water/.

50 "The Hidden Water We Use." *National Geographic*, environment.nationalgeographic. com/environment/freshwater/embedded-water/.

51 "Water Crisis - Learn About the Global Water Crisis." Water.org. water.org/our-impact/water-crisis/.

52 "Water Scarcity." World Wildlife Fund. www. worldwildlife.org/threats/water-scarcity.

53 "Water for Life Decade: Water Scarcity." United Nations Department of Economic and Social Affairs (UNDESA). www.un.org/ waterforlifedecade/scarcity.shtml.

54 "Consumer Information." North Carolina Potato Association. www.ncagr.gov/markets/ commodit/horticul/potatoes/facts.htm.

55 "Water for Life Decade: Water Scarcity." United Nations Department of Economic and Social Affairs (UNDESA). www.un.org/ waterforlifedecade/scarcity.shtml.

56 "U.S. Could Feed 800 Million People with Grain That Livestock Eat, Cornell Ecologist Advises Animal Scientists." *Cornell Chronicle* (August 7, 1997). news.cornell.edu/stories/1997/08/ us-could-feed-800-million-people-grain-livestock-eat.

57 "2016 World Hunger and Poverty Facts and Statistics." *Hunger Notes*. World Hunger Education Service. www.worldhunger. org/2015-world-hunger-and-poverty-facts-and-statistics/.

58 "Plant Uses / Edible." *Plants for a Future*. www. pfaf.org/user/edibleuses.aspx.

59 "Plant Uses / Edible." *Plants for a Future*. www. pfaf.org/user/edibleuses.aspx.

60 "What Is Happening to Agrobiodiversity?" FAO. www.fao.org/docrep/007/y5609e/ y5609e02.htm.

61 "What Is Happening to Agrobiodiversity?" FAO. www.fao.org/docrep/007/y5609e/ y5609e02.htm.

62 "World Hunger Statistics." *Statistic Brain*. www. statisticbrain.com/world-hunger-statistics/.

63 Foley, Jonathan. "A Five-Step Plan to Feed the World." *National Geographic*, www. nationalgeographic.com/foodfeatures/feeding-9-billion/.

64 Gold, Mark. *The Global Benefits of Eating Less Meat: A Report for Compassion in World Farming Trust*. Navodanya in Collaboration with Compassion in World Farming Trust (2004).

65 West, Paul C. "Leverage Points for Improving Global Food Security and the Environment." *Science* (July 18, 2014). www.science. sciencemag.org/content/345/6194/325, doi: 10.1126/science.1246067

66 Zelman, Kathleen M. "The Benefits of Vitamin C." WebMD. www.webmd.com/diet/features/ the-benefits-of-vitamin-c#1.

67 Ware, Megan. "Magnesium: Health Benefits, Sources, and Risks." *Medical News Today* (September 25, 2017). www. medicalnewstoday.com/articles/286839.php.

68 "Phytochemicals: Those Other Substances." *Berkeley Wellness* (May 1, 2014). www. berkeleywellness.com/healthy-eating/ nutrition/article/what-are-phytochemicals.

69 Schwartz, Madeline. "Deadly Riots in Venezuela Bring Food Shortage to Global Stage." *Global Citizen* (June 21, 2016). www.globalcitizen.org/ en/content/venezuela-hunger-crisis-conflict/.

70 McNally, Jess. "Can Vegetarianism Save the World? Nitty-gritty." *Stanford Magazine* (January/February 2010). https://alumni.stanford.edu/get/page/magazine/article/?article_id=29892.

71 Based on annual poultry consumption of 99 pounds in the U.S. per capita, the highest of all meat consumption. Beef is second at 53.8 pounds per year. Pork is last at 45.9 pounds per year. It takes 20 pounds of grain to produce 1 pound of meat, 7 pounds of grain to produce 1 pound of pork, and 5 pounds of grain to produce 1 pound of poultry. Altogether, it comes to 1,892 (given per capita consumption in the U.S.).

72 Assuming that if you are vegetarian, you save enough grain to feed 445 people every year.

73 "Quantifying the Environmental Benefits of Skipping the Meat." *ScienceDaily* (April 4, 2016). www.sciencedaily.com/releases/2016/04/160404170427.htm.

74 "Key Facts and Findings." FAO. www.fao.org/news/story/en/item/197623/icode/.

75 Good, Kate. "Stop the Oil Rigs! Study States We Have to Keep Fossil Fuels in Ground before 2050." *One Green Planet* (January 8, 2015). www.onegreenplanet.org/news/we-have-to-keep-fossil-fuels-in-ground/.

76 "Atmospheric CO2 Emissions." Carbon Accounting Systems. carbon-accounting.com/atmospheric-co2-emissions.

77 "Climate Change Is Making the World's Animals Really Sad ... Can We Cheer Them Up?" *One Green Planet* (December 16, 2014). www.onegreenplanet.org/animalsand-nature/climate-change-is-making-the-worlds-animals-really-sad/.

78 Algar, Jim. "California Pika Population in Decline, Researchers Blame Climate Change." *Tech Times* (February 3, 2015). www.techtimes.com/articles/30590/20150203/california-pika-population-in-decline-researchers-blame-climate-change.htm.

79 "Facts on Animal Farming and the Environment." *One Green Planet* (December 17, 2014). www.onegreenplanet.org/animalsandnature/facts-on-animal-farming-and-the-environment/.

80 Starrs, Tom. "Fossil Food: Consuming Our Future." Ecoliteracy.org. www.ecoliteracy.org/article/fossil-food-consuming-our-future.

81 Gerber, P.J. et al. "Tackling Climate Change Through Livestock: A Global Assessment of Emissions and Mitigation Opportunities." Food and Agriculture Organization of the United Nations (FAO): Rome (2013). www.fao.org/docrep/018/i3437e/i3437e.pdf.

82 "Livestock's Long Shadow: Environmental Issues and Options." FAO (2006). ftp://ftp.fao.org/docrep/fao/010/a0701e/a0701e04.pdf.

83 Good, Kate. "Coalition Slams EPA With Lawsuit for Letting Factory Farms Pollute the Planet." *One Green Planet* (January 28, 2015). www.onegreenplanet.org/news/coalition-sues-epa-over-factory-farm-pollution/.

84 "Energy and Food Production." *Eating Sustainability: An Introduction to Sustainable Food.* Emory University, Sustainability Initiatives (April 2010). sustainability.emory.edu/uploads/press/2015/04/2015041215581794/InfoSheet-Energy26FoodProduction.pdf.

85 "Farms and Land in Farms 2016 Summary." USDA (February 2017). usda.mannlib.cornell.edu/usda/current/FarmLandIn/FarmLandIn-02-17-2017.pdf.

86 U.S. Energy Information Administration

87 Casper, Julie Kerr. *Climate Systems: Interactive Forces of Global Warming* (Facts on File: New York), 165.

88 Good, Kate. "Serious About Addressing Climate Change? It's Time to Get Serious About Changing Your Diet." (September 8, 2014). www.onegreenplanet.org/animalsandnature/serious-about-addressing-climate-change-your-diet/.

89 Pimentel, David and Marcia Pimentel. "Sustainability of Meat-Based and Plant-Based Diets and the Environment." *The American Journal of Clinical Nutrition* (September 1, 2003). ajcn.nutrition.org/content/78/3/660S.full.

90 "Energy and Food Production." *Eating Sustainability: An Introduction to Sustainable Food.* Emory University, Sustainability Initiatives (April 2010). sustainability.emory.edu/uploads/press/2015/04/2015041215581794/InfoSheet-Energy26FoodProduction.pdf.

91 "Factory Farm Map." Food & Water Watch. factoryfarmmap.org/.

92   DeWeerdt, Sarah. "Is Local Food Better?" Worldwatch Institute. www.worldwatch.org/node/6064.

93   "The Real Deal on Compact Flourescent Light Bulbs." National Audobon Society. www.audubon.org/sites/default/files/documents/CFLs.pdf

94   Cobb, Jeff. "America's Lowest Carbon Footprint Cars." HybridCars.com (July 9, 2015). www.hybridcars.com/americas-lowest-carbon-footprint-cars/.

95   Goodland, Robert and Jeff Anhang. "Livestock and Climate Change." *World Watch*. Worldwatch Institute (November 2009). https://www.worldwatch.org/files/pdf/Livestock%20and%20Climate%20Change.pdf.

96   Gerber, P.J. et al. "Tackling Climate Change Through Livestock: A Global Assessment of Emissions and Mitigation Opportunities." Food and Agriculture Organization of the United Nations (FAO): Rome (2013). www.fao.org/docrep/018/i3437e/i3437e.pdf.

97   Goodland, Robert and Jeff Anhang. "Livestock and Climate Change." *World Watch*. Worldwatch Institute (November 2009). www.worldwatch.org/files/pdf/Livestock%20and%20Climate%20Change.pdf.

98   "Time to Get Real and Ditch That Hamburger, Because Cows Don't Belong in the Rainforest." *One Green Planet* (December 16, 2014). www.onegreenplanet.org/animalsandnature/burgers-cows-livestock-rainforest-destruction/.

99   "BUSTED! The 6 Worst Myths About Global Climate Change." *One Green Planet* (December 17, 2014). www.onegreenplanet.org/animalsandNOTES155nature/the-5-worst-myths-about-global-climate-change-busted/.

100   "Each Trip on the MTA Keeps More Than 10 Lbs. of Carbon Out of the Air." MTA. www.mta.info/news/2012/04/22/each-trip-mta-keeps-more-10-lbs-carbon-out-air.

101   Carrington, Damian. "Eating Less Meat Essential to Curb Climate Change, Says Report." *The Guardian* (December 2, 2014). www.theguardian.com/environment/2014/dec/03/eating-less-meat-curb-climate-change.

102   "Changing Global Diets Is Vital to Reducing Climate Change." Phys.org (August 31, 2014).

phys.org/news/2014-08-global-diets-vital-climate.html.

103   Loughry, Maryanne and Jane McAdam. "Kiribati: Relocation and Adaptation." *Forced Migration Review* 31 (October 2008). www.fmreview.org/climatechange/loughry-mcadam.html.

104   Milman, Oliver and Mae Ryan. "Sea Level Rise Is Already Driving People from the Marshall Islands." *Wired* (June 3, 2017). www.wired.com/2016/09/sea-level-rise-already-driving-people-marshall-islands/.

105   Chauvin, Rémi and Eric Hillaire. "Climate Change in the Marshall Islands and Kiribati, Before and After (Interactive)." *The Guardian* (March 11, 2015). www.theguardian.com/environment/ng-interactive/2015/mar/11/climate-change-in-the-marshall-islands-and-kiribati-before-and-after-interactive.

106   Riebeek, Holli. "The Carbon Cycle." Earth Observatory. NASA (June 16, 2011). earthobservatory.nasa.gov/Features/CarbonCycle/page5.php.

107   Springmann, Marco et al. "Analysis and Valuation of the Health and Climate Change Cobenefits of Dietary Change." *Proceedings of the National Academy of Sciences* 113:15 (April 12, 2016). National Acad Sciences. www.pnas.org/content/113/15/4146.

108   According to scientists, the key is to keep the climate from not exceeding the 2 degrees Celsius above preindustrial levels. If we can slow down the rate of climate change, we can prevent such weather events and thereby not have to face the worst consequences of extreme climate change.

109   Thornton, Philip et al. "Livestock and Climate Change." International Livestock Research Institute (November 2011). https://cgspace.cgiar.org/bitstream/handle/10568/10601/IssueBrief3.pdf.

110   Reilly, Kathleen. *Explore Soil!* (White River Junction, Vermont: Nomad Press, 2015), p. 50.

111   "What to Do with All of the Poo?" *Modern Farmer* (May 10, 2016). modernfarmer.com/2014/08/manure-usa/.

112   "Counting Chickens." *The Economist* (July 27, 2011). www.economist.com/blogs/dailychart/2011/07/global-livestock-counts.

113   Hauter, Wenonah. "New Data Shows Factory Farms Are a #LoadOfCrap." Food

& Water Watch (September 25, 2015). www. foodandwaterwatch.org/news/new-data-shows-factory-farms-are-loadofcrap.

114 Bardroff, Jenna. "The Dangers of Using Waste from Factory Farms as Fertilizer." *One Green Planet* (May 18, 2015). www.onegreenplanet. org/environment/the-dangers-of-using-waste-from-factory-farms-as-fertilizer/.

115 www.nyu.edu/sustainability/pdf/Fossil%2520F uel%2520and%2520Energy%2520Use%25202 %2520FCSummit-HO-20091207.pdf

116 "Waste Management." GRACE Communications Foundation, www.sustainabletable.org/906/waste-management.

117 "Air Quality." GRACE Communications Foundation. www.sustainabletable.org/266/air-quality.

118 Hribar, Carrie. "Understanding Concentrated Animal Feeding Operations and Their Impact on Communities." *Environmental Health* (2010). www.cdc.gov/nceh/ehs/docs/understanding_cafos_nalboh.pdf.

119 Hribar, Carrie. "Understanding Concentrated Animal Feeding Operations and Their Impact on Communities." *Environmental Health* (2010). www.cdc.gov/nceh/ehs/docs/understanding_cafos_nalboh.pdf.

120 Hribar, Carrie. "Understanding Concentrated Animal Feeding Operations and Their Impact on Communities." *Environmental Health* (2010). www.cdc.gov/nceh/ehs/docs/understanding_cafos_nalboh.pdf.

121 "Fish Finder." FAO, Fisheries & Aquaculture Department. www.fao.org/fishery/species/2917/ en.

122 Ford, Jennifer S. and Ransom A. Myers. "A Global Assessment of Salmon Aquaculture Impacts on Wild Salmonids." *PLoS Bio* (February 12, 2008). doi: 10.1371/journal. pbio.0060033.

123 Clover, Charles. "Pollution from Fish Farms 'as Bad as Sewage'." *The Telegraph* (September 19, 2000). www.telegraph.co.uk/news/ uknews/1355936/Pollution-from-fish-farms-as-bad-as-sewage.html.

124 "The Last of the Fish Cages Leave Eilat!" *Israel Water Blog* (July 9, 2008). zalul.wordpress. com/2008/06/12/the-last-of-the-fish-cages-leave-eilat/.

125 "Agricultural Waste Management Field Handbook." USDA, Natural Resources Conservation Service. www.nrcs.usda.gov/ wps/portal/nrcs/detailfull/national/technical/ ecoscience/mnm/?cid=stelprdb1045935.

126 Good, Kate. "These 10 Shocking Facts on Factory Farms and Water Pollution Will Make You Rethink That Burger." *One Green Planet* (June 22, 2017). www.onegreenplanet.org/ environment/shocking-facts-on-how-factory-farms-cause-water-pollution/.

127 "Pollution from Giant Livestock Farms Threatens Public Health." Institute for Agriculture and Trade Policy (July 25, 2001). www.iatp.org/news/pollution-from-giant-livestock-farms-threatens-public-health.

128 NOAA. "What is A Dead Zone?" U.S. Department of Commerce, National Ocean Service, 10 October 2017, oceanservice.noaa. gov/facts/deadzone.html.

129 "Is Meat Sustainable?" *World Watch* 17:4 (July/ August 2004). Worldwatch Institute. www. worldwatch.org/node/549.

130 Schechinger, Anne W. "How to Stop Farm Runoff from Spreading Dead Zones." *AgMag* (August 14, 2015). www.ewg.org/ agmag/2015/08/how-stop-farm-runoff-spreading-dead-zones.

131 Good, Kate. "These 10 Shocking Facts on Factory Farms and Water Pollution Will Make You Rethink That Burger." *One Green Planet* (June 22, 2017). www.onegreenplanet.org/ environment/shocking-facts-on-how-factory-farms-cause-water-pollution/.

132 Biello, David. "Oceanic Dead Zones Continue to Spread." *Scientific American* (August 15, 2008). www.scientificamerican.com/article/oceanic-dead-zones-spread/.

133 "Dead Zones." Virginia Institute of Marine Science. www.vims.edu/research/topics/ dead_zones/.

134 NASA. eoimages.gsfc.nasa.gov/images/ imagerecords/44000/44677/dead_zones_lrg. jpg.

135 Gallagher, James. "Farmers Urged to Cut Antibiotic Use." *BBC News* (December 8, 2015). www.bbc.com/news/health-35030262.

136 "If the Ocean Dies, We All Die!" Sea Shepherd Conservation Society (September 29, 2015). www.seashepherd.org/news-and-commentary/ commentary/if-the-ocean-dies-we-all-die.html.

137   Laurance, William F. et al. "Predictors of Deforestation in the Brazilian Amazon." *Journal of Biogeography* 29:5–6, pp. 737–748 (May 2002). doi: 10.1046/j.1365-2699.2002.00721.x.

138   Boucher, Doug. "10% of Greenhouse Gas Emissions Come from Deforestation." Union of Concerned Scientists (December 12, 2013). blog.ucsusa.org/doug-boucher/ten-percent-of-greenhouse-gas-emissions-come-from-deforestation-342.

139   "Climate Change and the Amazon Rainforest." *Amazon Watch*. amazonwatch.org/work/climate-change-and-the-amazon-rainforest.

140   Wallace, Scott. "Amazon Rain Forest, Deforestation, Forest Conservation - National Geographic Magazine." *National Geographic*. environment.nationalgeographic.com/environment/habitats/last-of-amazon/.

141   "Cattle and Conservation: The Amazon's First Sustainable Cattle Ranch." *Rainforest Alliance* (September 22, 2014). www.rainforest-alliance.org/articles/cattle-conservation-brazil.

142   Veiga, J. B. et al. "Cattle Ranching in the Amazon Rainforest." FAO, XII World Forestry Congress (2003). www.fao.org/docrep/ARTICLE/WFC/XII/0568-B1.HTM.

143   "Slaughtering the Amazon." Greenpeace (June 1, 2009). www.greenpeace.org/international/en/publications/reports/slaughtering-the-amazon/.

144   "Soy, You & Deforestation." WWF. wwf.panda.org/what_we_do/footprint/agriculture/soy/consumers/.

145   "Brazil to Overtake U.S. as World's Top Meat Exporter." Globalmeatnews.com (August 15, 2016). www.globalmeatnews.com/Article/2016/08/16/Brazil-to-sprint-past-US-in-meat-production.

146   "Environmental & Social Impacts of Soy." WWF. wwf.panda.org/what_we_do/footprint/agriculture/soy/impacts/.

147   Butler, Rhett. "Medicinal Plants." Mongabay.com (July 22, 2012). rainforests.mongabay.com/1007.htm.

148   Cronin, Aisling Maria. "Documentary Exposing the Causes of the World's 6th Mass Extinction of Animals Premiers in Theaters!" *One Green Planet* (September 21, 2015). www.onegreenplanet.org/news/racing-extinction-premiers-in-theaters/.

149   "Living Planet Report 2016. Risk and Resilience in a New Era." WWF (2016). awsassets.panda.org/downloads/lpr_living_planet_report_2016.pdf.

150   "Extinctions during Human Era Worse than Thought." Brown University (September 2, 2014). news.brown.edu/articles/2014/09/extinctions.

151   Williams, Mark et al. "The Anthropocene Biosphere." *The Anthropocene Review* (June 18, 2015). journals.sagepub.com/doi/abs/10.1177/2053019615591020.

152   Zalasiewicz, Jan. "Scale and Diversity of the Physical Technosphere: A Geological Perspective." *The Anthropocene Review* (November 28, 2016). journals.sagepub.com/doi/pdf/10.1177/2053019616677743.

153   University of Plymouth. "New Study Reveals the Global Impact of Debris on Marine Life." *EurekAlert!* (February 19, 2015). www.eurekalert.org/pub_releases/2015-02/uop-nsr021915.php.

154   Dolmage, Jaimi. "Time to get Real and Ditch That Hamburger, Because Cows Don't Belong in the Rainforest." *One Green Planet* (September 17, 2014). www.onegreenplanet.org/animalsandnature/burgers-cows-livestock-rainforest-destruction/.

155   "Appetite for Destruction." WWF-UK (October 3, 2017). www.wwf.org.uk/updates/appetite-for-destruction.

156   "How Eating Meat Hurts Wildlife and the Planet." Take Extinction Off Your Plate. www.takeextinctionoffyourplate.com/meat_and_wildlife.html.

157   "Grazing Cattle: The New 'Invasive Species.'" *One Green Planet* (November 13, 2015). www.onegreenplanet.org/animalsandnature/grazing-cattle-the-new-invasive-species/.

158   Dolmage, Jaimi. "Time to get Real and Ditch That Hamburger, Because Cows Don't Belong in the Rainforest." *One Green Planet* (September 17, 2014). www.onegreenplanet.org/animalsandnature/burgers-cows-livestock-rainforest-destruction/.

159   Good, Kate. "The Truth about the Federal Wildlife Service: Here to Protect Animals or Paying Interests?" *One Green Planet* (June 2, 2014). www.onegreenplanet.org/animalsand-nature/the-truth-about-the-federal-wildlife-service-here-to-protect-animal-or-paying-interests/.

160 Estrada, Orietta C. "What Is Happening with America's Gray Wolves And How You Can Protect Them." *One Green Planet* (November 13, 2015). www.onegreenplanet.org/animalsand-nature/what-is-happening-with-americas-gray-wolves-and-how-you-can-protect-them/.

161 "Grazing." Center for Biological Diversity. www.biologicaldiversity.org/programs/public_lands/grazing/.

162 Pasolini, Antonio. "The Amazon Wants You . . . to Stop Eating Meat." *One Green Planet* (July 13, 2012). www.onegreenplanet.org/animalsandnature/the-amazon-wants-you-to-stop-eating-meat/.

163 Good, Kate. "What Does Eating Beef Have to Do with Species Extinction?" *One Green Planet* (December 16, 2014). www.onegreenplanet.org/animalsandnature/cattle-ranching-jaguars-species-extinction-and-the-amazon/.

164 Urban, Mark C. "Accelerating Extinction Risk from Climate Change." *Science* (May 1, 2015). American Association for the Advancement of Science. science.sciencemag.org/content/348/6234/571.full.

165 Myers, Ransom A. and Boris Worm. "Rapid Worldwide Depletion of Predatory Fish Communities." *Nature* 423, 280-283 (May 15, 2003). doi:10.1038/nature01610

166 Worm, Boris et al. "Impacts of Biodiversity Loss on Ocen Ecosystem Services." *Science* 314:5800, pp 787–790 (November 3, 2006). doi: 10.1126/science.1132294.

167 Pepelko, Kristina. "The Destructive Nature of Deep Sea Trawling (Infographic)." *One Green Planet* (November 21, 2013). www.onegreenplanet.org/animalsandnature/the-destructive-nature-of-deep-sea-trawling-infographic/.

168 Mathiesen, Karl. "World's Oceans Facing Biggest Coral Die-off in History, Scientists Warn." *The Guardian* (October 8, 2015). www.theguardian.com/environment/2015/oct/08/worlds-oceans-facing-biggest-coral-die-off-in-history-scientists-warn.

169 Goudarzi, Sara. "Quarter of Species Gone by 2050." *LiveScience* (April 11, 2006). www.livescience.com/4056-quarter-species-2050.html.

170 Pratt, Sarah. "The Flowers Miss the Bees." *New Trail* (April 4, 2016). www.ualberta.ca/newtrail/spring-2016/features-dept/the-flowers-miss-the-bees.

171 "Pollinators" U.S. Fish and Wildlife Service. www.fws.gov/pollinators/pollinatorpages/aboutpollinators.html.

172 Kleijn, David et al. "Delivery of Crop Pollination Services Is an Insufficient Argument for Wild Pollinator Conservation." *Nature Communications* 6 (June 16, 2105). www.nature.com/articles/ncomms8414. doi: doi:10.1038/ncomms8414

173 Monks, Kieron. "Wild Supercows Return to Europe." *CNN* (January 9, 2017). www.cnn.com/2017/01/09/world/auroch-rewilding/index.html.

174 "The Impossible Burger." Impossible Foods. impossiblefoods.com/.

175 "Quantifying the Environmental Benefits of Skipping the Meat." *ScienceDaily* (April 4, 2016). www.sciencedaily.com/releases/2016/04/160404170427.htm.

Nil: My parents, Mathew and Vicky Zacharias, have always encouraged me to follow my own path and ingrained in me the core principles of discipline, hard work, and honesty. Without their love and support I would not have had the freedom to explore my various passions while staying firmly grounded. They encouraged me to put my thoughts down on paper (and my bedroom walls!), in the form of words and images, at a very young age, and that habit shaped the course of my entire life, from writing poems and short stories in school to exploring the graphic arts and music in my teens, law school, and every career choice that led up to me writing this, my first book. I can't thank them enough for everything.

I'd also like to mention the entire team at One Green Planet. Without their hard work and passion, onegreeplanet.org never could have succeeded as it has. Thank you so much!

Gene: I'd like to thank Nick Bromley for his incredible research, writing, and guidance; Mark Langley for his excellent editorial suggestions; and Miranda Spencer, who improves every book I write. Thanks also go to Kathy Freston, who is always ready to give advice whenever it's needed. And, as always and ever, Chris Hays.

We would both like to add our thanks to our four-legged companions. Nil must mention his rescue dog, Goji, who helps remind him every day to live in the present moment stopping to enjoy a treat or play fetch!). Likewise, Gene has to mention Gus and Julia, two beautiful rescue cats, and Friday and Toby, two wonderful rescue dogs, who may not always eat for the planet, but who would save the world in a minute if they could.

Both of us are very grateful to Peter McGuigan, our tireless agent at Foundry; Kate Good for her reliable and relentless research support; and the team at Abrams who believed that this book needed to be published and trusted in the vision we had for its content and format. Samantha Weiner has been a terrific editor, Najeebah Al-Ghadban's design helped create an important dialogue, and Annalea Manalili's attention to detail ensured that nothing got lost in the process.

Additionally, we'd like to say a big thank you to Lily Chow, whose illustrations bring these facts and figures to life, and Katie Gaffney, Kimberly Sheu, and Jennifer Bastien who helped put the book together and bring it into the world.

We'd also like to thank all the researchers, scientists, and experts who have dedicated their professional lives to studying the devastating impact of our industrialized food system on the environment. There are far too many of you to name here, but without your work, we would never have woken up to the real impact of our food choices, and we would have lacked the arsenal of compelling facts and statistics that form the bedrock of this book.

Nil Zacharias is the co-founder of One Green Planet (OneGreenPlanet.org), the leading independent media company focused on food sustainability. He is also host of the popular weekly podcast, "#EatForThePlanet with Nil Zacharias."

Gene Stone has written many books on plant-based nutrition and animal protection, including the #1 *New York Times* bestseller *Forks Over Knives*. He has also cowritten the bestsellers *How Not to Die*, *The Engine 2 Diet*, and *Living the Farm Sanctuary Life*.